The F

Other Works by Fred Harrison include

2010: The Inquest (2010)
The Silver Bullet (2008)
Wheels of Fortune (2006)
Ricardo's Law: House Prices and the Great Tax Clawback Scam (2006)
Boom Bust: House Prices, Banking and the Depression of 2010 (2005; 2nd edn 2010)
The Chaos Makers (1997, with Frederic J.Jones)
The Power in the Land (1983)

The Predator Culture
The Roots and Intent
of Organised Violence

FRED HARRISON

SHEPHEARD-WALWYN (PUBLISHERS) LTD

© 2010 Fred Harrison

All rights reserved. No part of this book may be
reproduced in any form without the written permission
of the publisher, Shepheard-Walwyn (Publishers) Ltd

First published in 2010 by
Shepheard-Walwyn (Publishers) Ltd
107 Parkway House, Sheen Lane
London SW14 8LS

British Library Cataloguing in Publication Data
A catalogue record of this book
is available from the British Library

ISBN-13: 978-0-85683-273-4

Typeset by Arthouse Publishing Solutions,
Alderton, Suffolk
Printed and bound through
s|s| media limited, Wallington, Surrey

Contents

Acknowledgements vi
Prologue: The Failed State vii

Part 1: A General Theory of Violence
1 The Spatial Dynamics of Evolution 3
2 The Culture of Pauperisation 15
3 The Socio-Ecology of Peace: Costa Rica 27

Part 2: The Social Pathology of Land Grabs
4 Colonialism & the Corruption of People Power 43
5 The Pathology of Re-ordered Space 57
6 Genocide & the Concentration Camp 69

Part 3: Structures of Violence
7 Neo-colonialism & the Dysfunctional State 83
8 Fascism: Italy's Fourth Shore 95
9 Economics of the Covenant 107

Part 4: Healing Humanity
10 Freedom through Taxation 121
11 Truth and Reconciliation 135
12 Principles of Non-violent Governance 147

Bibliography 157
About the Author 165
Index 167

Acknowledgments

This study into what (frankly) has been a painful excursion into the dark side of history was made possible by a grant from theIU, a UN-affiliated think-tank which has the courage to venture into areas where other NGOs fear to tread. That claim may be tested by reviewing its website (*www.theiu.org*). My thanks for their trenchant comments on an early draft are due to Edward Dodson and Dave Wetzel.

Prologue
The Failed State

VIOLENCE is one of the currencies of capitalism. It is used to transact what we shall identify as a need of this social system, in the way that money and credit are employed to oil the wheels of the economy. As such, this violence is intentional and inextricably bound up with the laws and institutions which constitute the foundations of capitalism. Organised violence, therefore, cannot be excised in response to moral sentiments that are offended by its consequences.

Collectively, we have grown to accept that some of the results of this violence *are* acceptable. If we wish to modify the violent approach to transacting the needs of capitalism, we must understand its nature, if we are to identify the barriers that are erected against reform.

There are two kinds of violence. The first is visible, where the intent is known or can be identified. The invasion of Saddam Hussein's Iraq was portrayed by the Bush/Blair alliance as humanitarian in its intent. Or was it because capitalism needed to take control of that country's oil fields?

The second form of violence is applied covertly. In some of these cases, even the decision-makers do not understand the consequences of their actions. Thus, under the guise of what appears to be a non-violent programme, the outcome may be the creation of circumstances that unleash violence. An example of this is one of the first decisions taken by Barack Obama when he became President of the US. He wanted to invoke a peaceful approach to help Pakistan, whose badlands between Pakistan and its porous border with Afghanistan were "the most dangerous place in the world".

Characterising a place in these terms assigns responsibility for violence. I will explain that, in terms of the violence that now confronts us in the 21st century, the actual "crucible of terror" (British Prime Minister Gordon Brown's term for the Pakistan/Afghan region), is situated in the West. It is embedded in the laws and policies that we take for granted as forces for good rather than evil. As will become apparent in *The Predator Culture*, the US tax dollars that Obama promised to pour into Pakistan's infrastructure will foster the conditions on the ground that nurture the discontent which lead to violence.

I question the cherished beliefs that were incubated in the age that we label the Enlightenment. Just how enlightened were some of the values and institutions that Europe visited on itself, and then on the rest of the world, will be questioned, to identify what drives socially organised violence.

I advance a theory that explains this violence in terms of a particular set of property rights. Historically, the main intent behind the major events of violence has been the quest to appropriate other people's land, or the resources of nature in and on that land. The main driver is not the idiosyncratic psychology of personal greed, but the propensities driven by institutions that rely on the privatisation of the income from land.

To understand how capitalism gives rise to organised violence, we need to appreciate that two distinct cultures are forced to co-habit the same space. Critics on the Left pretend that capitalism is a homogenous system, to be vilified without qualification. But the problems stem from one of the pillars of capitalism. The *Predator* culture represents the set of values and activities that feed off the income generated by others. Co-existing with the predators are the *Producers*. They are unwilling partners in this relationship, obliged for historical reasons to serve as the host body to which the predators, as parasites, cling. Classical economic concepts differentiated these two categories. Today, however, because of the manipulation of key words (particularly, *rent*) under the influence of what became the post-classical school of economics, it has become difficult even for scholars to comprehend those contours of capitalism that are worth retaining, and those that need to be exorcised (see Box 1).

We need analytical concepts that reflect realities on the ground. Medical metaphors help. My focus is on the *sociogenic* structure of society. By this, I mean the foundation laws, and especially those that relate to property rights.

In monitoring the violence that *had* to be deployed to establish the principal institutions of western society, I attempt to demonstrate that it was the intolerable stresses within capitalism that provoked the sociogenic *shift* into variations on that violent theme, such as fascism and communism. These were attempts to create competing systems which (we now know) could not be tolerated by the capitalism from which they were incubated.

Box 1: The Dynamics of Land Grabbing

As defined by classical economists, Labour is rewarded with wages. Thus, one's appetite and lifestyle is constrained by the productivity that goes into value-adding work. Those who hold the title deeds to land receive rent. Rent is not earned income. It is a transfer payment from those who work for their living.

For the owners of land, appetite and lifestyle is unbounded. Since I do not labour for my income (as rent-receiver) I can sit back and enjoy the fruits of the labours of others. But how else can I occupy myself, other than by expanding my consumption? There are no limits to gluttony. For the landed magnates of old, one palace was not enough. Henry VIII did not just collect wives. Having grabbed the lands of England's monasteries, his appetite extended to the construction of five palaces and 50 opulent country homes.

Landlords needed to control the state, to protect their privileges. But what happens when the land within one's nation, once held in common, has been enclosed and privatised? The only way to assuage unbounded lust was to embark on colonial conquest. Thus, the application of violence within the home territory was inflicted on others in the course of territorial appropriation.

But in addition, there are sub-groups within capitalism that rely on defensive mechanisms based on a reciprocal violence. They emerge through sociogenic *drifts*. A notable example is the way in which the household economy may metamorphose into the Mafia: one defensive mechanism that arose from the displacement of people from their natural habitats.

These drifts and shifts imply that some natural state of affairs exists in which the social organisation achieves stability: equilibrium, in the language of economics, or *sustainability* in the language of the ecologist. Capitalism offends this ideal state of affairs. Its dualistic constitution guarantees a permanent state of economic warfare between Predators and Producers. These two uniquely different forms of culture co-exist only because of violence, the application of which ranges from the subtle to the nakedly coercive.

Why we are all Complicit

GOVERNMENTS co-opt all of us into sharing responsibility for the exercise of violence against others. How this happens becomes apparent when we analyse the tax system. Take the case of the US President's plan to spend $7.5bn on upgrading Pakistan's infrastructure, such as its highways.

The President's advisers failed to tell Obama that the investment of US tax dollars in a community's shared services would drive many people even deeper into despair – and render them vulnerable to extremists who kill in the name of God. So in announcing his plan on March 17, 2009, to spend $1.5bn every year, for five years, the president really believed in his "focused goal: to disrupt, dismantle and defeat Al-Qaeda in Pakistan and Afghanistan". In reality, *on the ground*, that money drives up the rents paid by tenant farmers, pushing more people off the land, adding to the stresses of life in the slums of Islamabad and Karachi, and exposing more youths to the attractions of suicidal revenge.

Land tenure is at the heart of the problem of Pakistan and Afghanistan's crumbling communities. Unwittingly, Obama's generosity intensifies the social divide, creating a crisis that is funded by unwitting American taxpayers.

President Obama is not the only person to commend a strategy that backfires in fatal ways. Anti-poverty campaigners are annexed to a doctrine of economic development which has similar outcomes. Pop singer Bob Geldof, for example, a champion of the poor, preaches the need to pour $50bn into Africa's infrastructure, to raise living standards and prevent avoidable deaths.[1] But the tax system prescribed by the West's economic doctrines has the opposite effect. Distortions directly attributable to an unbalanced tax code cause land prices to rise, working people to be displaced and poverty to be deepened. This outcome is not intended either by President Obama or Bob Geldof. But it is the Iron Law of Taxation.

The way that tax policies cause (or reinforce the resort to) organised violence, remains unanalysed by social scientists. The evidence is distressing, but it needs to be confronted. There is nothing in the animal kingdom to match the evil deeds of humans. Despite all the evidence to the contrary, however, we *can* eliminate the institutionalised violence that permeates our lives.

Violence, according to the editors of *On Violence*, "marks the new millennium; it registers as *the* sign of post-Cold War fever".[2] Some people share the view of William James, the 19th century American philosopher, who contended that "the plain truth is that people *want* war. They want it anyhow; for itself and apart from each and every possible consequence. It is the final bouquet of life's fireworks…Society would rot without the mystical blood-payment".[3] If this were really the case, there would be little hope for our species. If the gospel of despair cannot be challenged, the sensible goal of public policy would be to ensure that one's own society exercised superior force over others until the inevitable happened: the arrival of an even bigger bully on the block.

Resigning ourselves to the belief that violence is inevitable is a self-fulfilling prophesy. The violence we endure does not spring from the individual's perverse appetite for inflicting pain or destroying property. Rather, that violence is *systemic*, and it has its roots in a particular part of the structure on which our communities are built. If this is correct,

---

1 Geldof (2009).
2 Lawrence and Karim (2007: 3).
3 James (1926: 258)

we can identify the source of violence, and formulate the practical solution. The editors of *On Violence* would not agree. In their view, "There is no general theory of violence apart from its practices".[4] I contest this view.

Despite the acts of cruelty of which most of us are capable, as individuals we can't mobilise armies to trample over the territorial rights of others. For that, we need the power of the state. And the state has been structured to predispose our societies to acts of violence in all its forms.

To understand the roots and *intent* of systemic violence, we need to excavate deep into the anthropology of human evolution. Part I provides a framework within which to diagnose the history and dynamics of organised violence. The need for such a reassessment of the causes of socially organised violence is self-evident. The tools for the absolute destruction of life, as we humans have grown to know it, have been developed to the point where they can be miniaturised and deployed by small groups of fanatics. This makes it imperative that we agree to cease developing and using weapons of mass destruction. But such an agreement is not possible without a clear understanding of what animates systemic violence.

By examining the cultural and historical context of particular episodes of violence, we achieve a sense of why humans engage in exercises that lead to mass deaths. By following the clues, it becomes evident that the solution to a generalised – and sustainable – peace, is practical. That solution does not entail the redesign of human nature or the deployment of massive military "peace-keeping" forces. Rather, peace springs out of the rules that secure justice for everyone. In other words, we are not promoting a vision of utopia; rather, a workable formula for the prosperity to which every nation, and most individuals, are already committed.

The Language of Peace

THE ROLE of peace-making has been appropriated by western nations. They use democracy as the paradigm for trying to persuade adversaries

---

4 Lawrence and Karim (2007: 7).

to settle their disputes. This model is open to abuse not just by tyrants such as Robert Mugabe, but even by the US, as we saw in the case of the Florida procedures for re-electing George W. Bush to the White House. This has made it easy for authoritarian characters like Mugabe to justify their abusive behaviour by denigrating the values and institutions of democracy.

In Part IV, an approach based on the concepts of Truth and Reconciliation is identified as offering the starting point for renewal. This technique was used in South Africa once the apartheid regime had capitulated. Under the chairmanship of the then archbishop, Desmond Tutu, a commission catalogued the crimes committed by whites against blacks. The crimes were examined within a framework which enabled the two sides to reach an understanding of how to co-exist. The reconciliation was incomplete, however, because there was no resolution of the issue that brought the whites to Africa in the first place: land. Nonetheless, the viability of the truth and reconciliation approach was evident in that case, and it inspires the thought that it might be adapted to improve the tools at the disposal of communities that genuinely wish to live in peace.

The proposed reform to the structure of property rights is not a soft option. The West has many skeletons in its cupboard, requiring a humility on the part of its diplomats. Much of the violence in the world today is a legacy of Western state manipulation of other people's homelands. Therefore, if we are to eliminate systemic violence, the changes that need to be wrought in laws and institutions must challenge cherished ideas. Moral dilemmas will surface. The tragedy of Zimbabwe illustrates this difficulty. The West objects to Mugabe's thugs intruding on the properties of white farmers but, not so long ago, whites used thuggery to displace African tribes from their land.

Practical strategies are needed which are consistent with the dignity of everyone. A new approach to political philosophy is required to frame the strategies. Whereas the rule of law formalises social solidarity (as elaborated by French sociologist Emile Durkheim), the role of the law of property (as I will explain), when it privatises the benefits from land, necessarily has the opposite effect. People are divided, communities ruptured. The outcome is violence that manifests itself at all layers of existence:

- *Physically*, by excluding people from parts of the social space on which they depend for biological existence.
- *Mentally*, by subordinating people psychologically, separating them from the landscape which is integral to identity.
- *Socially*, by rupturing people from spaces their ancestors once considered sacred, which retain special significance even in a secular age.

We are here concerned with a weapon of mass destruction just as lethal as those being innovated in the laboratories of the disillusioned and the perverse. This study interrogates the *social process* that is the primary cause of the deaths of millions of people every year. In the literature on violence, they receive no more than fleeting references, such as the observation by Daniel Linotte that "oil rents could fund terrorism".[5]

Over the past four centuries, the privatisation of the rents of land and nature's resources was the key driver of systemic violence. The peace dividends that would flow from a general resolution to the contests over the ownership of those rents would dwarf the benefits from merely smothering conflicts within the current rules that govern nations. The material, psychological, social and spiritual benefits that would flow from the proposed shift in the structure of the public's finances are staggering.

Hitherto, there has been insufficient public pressure to identify the general solution to violence. After killing one or two million people, populations could recover and kick-start social renewal. But we have now reached the point at which we can terminate human life itself. So it is imperative that we place at the top of the political agenda the formula that would satisfy everyone in a way that finally banishes the need to resort to violence. But that is not as easy as one would imagine. Societies grounded in the principles of systemic violence are

---

5 Linotte, (2007: 272).

obliged to socialise their populations into thinking in ways that make them *accept* the abuse of nature, and the termination of the rights of others. The outcome may be called *trauma thinking*. Once locked into that thought-process, it becomes difficult to escape into new ways of viewing the world.

The notion of trauma as a response to a violent experience is currently confined to psycho-therapy. Even within this discipline, "the rediscovery of trauma as an etiological factor in mental disorders is only about 20 years old".[6] Shocking experiences – such as prolonged exposure to abuse in childhood, or bombardment in a military conflict – leave traces of a neuro-biological kind, which may dispose victims to self-harm, or violent acts against others.

Can the concept of trauma be applied to a society? If a population is left in a state of *dis*-ease as a result of its violent rupture from a supporting prop, might this manifest itself in a collective trauma? If the population is forced to adapt to a dysfunctional social environment, might that not lead to a distinctive way of thinking – traumatic thinking? Might this notion explain why people rationalise behaviour which we would not want to acknowledge as normal?

The notion of trauma may be important because it obliges us to specify what can be considered *normal*, or *healthy*. In an age of relativism, the idea of separating societies between those that are "normal", and others that are not normal, is avoided. But the need to define what we mean by a *healthy* society does oblige us to think about what is important in the fabric of social systems.

The starting point for these reflections must be the rules and institutions that were developed over tens of thousands of years. These provided the framework for action that made possible the human voyage of self discovery. Migration to all points between the polar ends of our planet was associated with the process of self-consciousness that integrated our species deeper into the ways of nature. We may take those social systems as benchmarks for *normality*. The customs and practices were enabling, providing support for the emerging imagination that made possible the experiments in ways of living

---

6 Schore (2003: 189).

without which our species could not have arrived at the gates of the first civilisations.

Europe's explorers and anthropologists of the 19th century classified pre-civilisation societies as primitive. We now know better. We acknowledge that early social systems were sophisticated mechanisms for integrating humans into their homelands. But when one of the key cultural pillars was undermined, whole populations were traumatised. Tracing the linkages provides us with a deeper appreciation of complex behaviour which otherwise seems perplexing (such as the resort to alcohol and the abuse of children) in those communities.

The notion of a traumatised society is resisted in the social sciences. In economics, the dominant model (now discredited by the financial crisis of 2008) portrayed market-based economic societies as self-regulating, operating rationally to secure optimum outcomes through the fluid interaction of component parts. This paradigm of a functional system was favoured over the past few decades, despite the history of cyclical breakdowns. But before economists abstracted their theorising from the spatial reality within which we all live, some analysts did recognise abnormal symptoms in Western communities. One of these was the French mathematician León Walras (1834-1910). On page 424 of *Etudes d'economie politique appliqué* (1898), he described the therapeutic benefits that would arise from the re-socialisation of land:

> The modern world would have cured its *social wound*, a thing that the ancient world could not accomplish.[7]

The Predator Culture identifies the roots of that social wound, analyses how the trauma festered in the interstices of European civilisation and spread its toxic virus throughout the world to asphyxiate the global community.

---

7 Italics added. I owe this reference to Fernando Scornick-Gerstein. See his *The Marginalists and the Special Status of Land as a Factor of Production* (forthcoming: 2010), co-authored with Fred Foldvary. Walras advocated the nationalization of land because he shared Adam Smith's view that the value of land would increase faster than other sources of income, and that rent would be sufficient to fund public expenditure without the need to resort to taxes on earned incomes.

Part 1
A General Theory of Violence

Man has lost the capacity to foresee and forestall... he will end up destroying the earth. — Albert Schweitzer

CHAPTER 1

THE SPATIAL DYNAMICS OF EVOLUTION

TO differentiate from other species – to gain a selective advantage over the control of resources – *homo sapiens* had to find a way of escaping from the iron laws of nature. Instincts – those laws in action – had to be complimented with, and where possible modified by, rules of behaviour that gave rise to culture.

In achieving this mission, humans accomplished something unique. A new dimension was added to the life processes on Earth. If Gaia is viewed as organic life in the biosphere, humans added the spiritual, intellectual and aesthetic dimensions that melded with nature to deliver the power to create. The interaction between humans and nature's resources made possible the overlaying of culture on the landscape.

To realise their creative potential, however, humans had to formalise the relationship with nature to make life possible beyond subsistence levels of existence. The crafting of the rules governing that relationship with land – the *rights of tenure* – was the primary contract on which everything else depended for humankind's journey through time and space.

Nature may be defined as the laws that enabled life to originate and differentiate into species, and for those species to co-exist within shared ecological niches. For species to survive, the biological rules had to ensure that life-sustaining resources were not depleted. Predators, for example, should not be wilful, wasteful destroyers of life. The limits on killing – on violent behaviour in general – should be constrained by reproductive need rather than by unchecked avarice. Feeding off the available life-generating resources had to be kept proportionate to the carrying capacity of stocks within the ecological niche. The biologically-based instincts which secure this balance were wrapped up in what ethologists call *territoriality*.

Humans as territorial creatures instinctively knew how to distribute their numbers in a balanced way to secure their ability to penetrate deep into evolutionary timescales. The universe they fashioned on Earth – the social universe – depended on the capacity to develop traditions which symbolically fused with, and then superseded, biological instincts. This gave humans a greater range of opportunities. Unlike the rules inherent in DNA-based instincts, the rules of culture were plastic. They could be adapted to meet the opportunities offered by new habitats, first as a result of extensive migration around the globe, then by the intensive use of resources on the home territory, through the advances of knowledge and technology. Early migratory groups, as they evolved into clans and tribes and settled on new territories, defined rules that secured a nurturing relationship with their habitats. This enabled them to peel back ever more layers of nature's riches, to expand the range of lifestyles.

Land rights, which determine the primary relationships, established the ethos of co-operation between individuals at both the material and social levels. The learning process was enriched through the interaction of biological need and the expansion of the universe of the mind that was nourished by the belief in life beyond the confines of Earth. The fusion of the material potential of the ecological niche with spiritual awareness expanded the opportunities within the social universe (Figure 1:1).

Humans continued to share their characteristics with other species. The differences were of degree, in terms of emotions, moral behaviour, the facility to create and use tools, the ability to deceive. But humans were a breed apart because of the capacity to contemplate, anticipate the outcomes of their actions, and articulate ideas that expanded the social universe beyond the material. They understood that there was the "greater good", and the supernatural. Thus, uniquely, humans created the concepts of religion, spirituality, and secular social behaviour grounded in

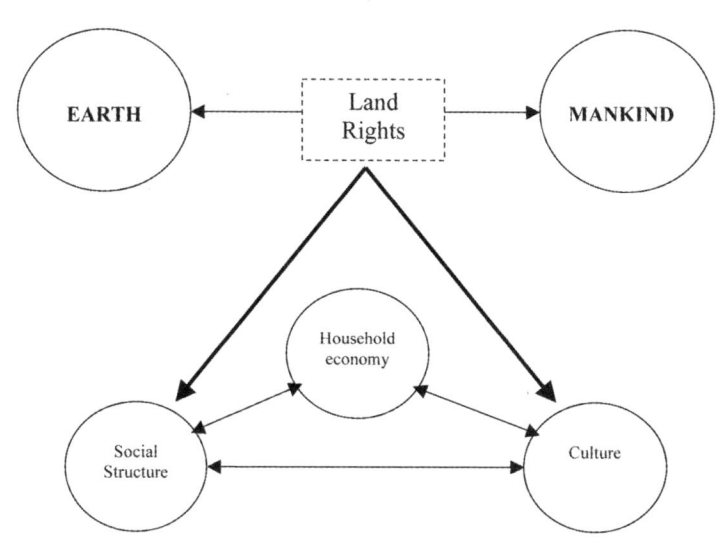

Figure 1:1 Structural Dynamics of the Social Universe

a moral framework. This singular facility required a unique imagination. It was central to the terms on which humans distributed themselves through space, by securing the veneration of nature and equalising the access rights of individuals within the bands that roamed in search of new habitats.[1] This spatial distribution fostered equality between people, rather than locking them into an hierarchical relationship. Egalitarianism was derived from the biological past but enshrined in the cultural future.

The structure of this social universe was comprised of three parts. First, the household economy was designed to meet biological needs. From gathering and hunting, and then growing food, people became conscious of the laws of nature. The scientific method (empiricism) was incubated within a folklore framework. Secondly, the social structure: lives were embedded within a formal system of traditions and rules that governed the behaviour of the individual within the group. The third dimension was culture, which encompassed the aesthetics of the new universe.

Culture in its content and scope varied to reflect the accessible resources. But the general rules remained consistent even as humans

---

1 Diamond (1971: 164-166).

fanned out around the globe on their journey of discovery. The non-negotiable philosophy underpinning the rules was the one that regulated interaction with Earth. As collective consciousness evolved – with the deepening of morality and intelligence – so culture could be expanded. But at no point could humans abandon their reliance on the integrity of the tenurial customs and laws that regulated their relationship with Earth. When they transgressed those rules, they paid a terrible price – extinction.[2] At all times, they needed to refine ancient wisdom to keep pace with the accumulating knowledge and technologies that expanded the reach of the social universe.

The Components of Social Labour

Figure 1:2 The Functional Distribution of Labour's Product

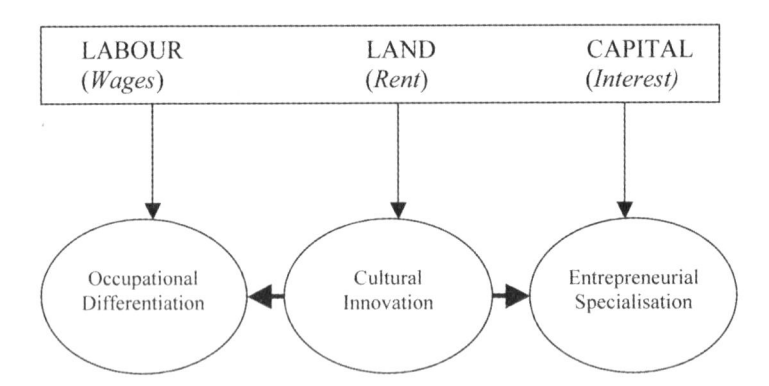

LABOUR (*Wages*)	LAND (*Rent*)	CAPITAL (*Interest*)
Occupational Differentiation	Cultural Innovation	Entrepreneurial Specialisation

The key element in the evolution from tribal formations to the earliest urban-based civilisations was the differentiation of the products of labour into their functional uses. The classical concepts of economics may be applied to classify the processes that culminated in achievements such as the city civilisations of Mesopotamia.

The *household economy* functioned as a self-supporting unit. A share of its product was retained to secure inter-generational survival. The reproductive function shaped the family life-cycle. The "wages" of labour defined the potential for differentiation within the groups, resulting in increasingly complex inter-personal relationships, roles

---

2 Diamond (2005).

for individuals (elders and spiritual leaders) and personal aspirations. Flowing from these interactions emerged the individual's morality, increasingly intense co-operation, and the formation of complex associations outside the household unit.

With settlement and the onset of pastoralism and agriculture, *occupational specialisation* flowed out of the accumulation of capital (cattel, derived from cattle), and the conceptualisation of an accumulation that we now call "interest".[3] Specialisation led to increasingly sophisticated technology and rituals that enriched workplace associations (such as guilds).[4]

Culture synthesised the potential of people and their technologies, facilitating the innovations in the religious life, secular authority and the arts. Spiritual life found its expression in the early paintings and carvings on rock faces; and the arts and sciences of production led to the reconfiguration of the landscape, real or imagined. The earliest city-civilisations remained egalitarian, their monuments reaching up to the heavens, celebrations of the religious or "other" life. These were funded out of the surplus which was worked out of Earth, resulting from the varying potential of each location for generating wealth, which we now call "rent".

Civilisation was possible because people agreed to disaggregate the product of their labour. That part which was consumed as wages or reinvested as interest – to reproduce themselves and their working tools – was distinguished from the surplus needed to nourish the cultural life. Culture was possible because of the capacity to both produce a surplus and to reserve it for the common welfare.[5] Today, we ascribe to that surplus the technical term *economic rent* (which we here designate as rent). People endowed their spiritual leaders with this rent to construct the monuments that expressed their spirituality. Priests were relieved of the need to work in the fields or workshops, to provide the sacred leadership that communities created to serve their

---

3 Diamond (1971: Part II).
4 Kropotkin (1987: Chs. 5-6).
5 That surplus was delivered in various forms, including labour services, or products worked out of the ground, or (in the later market economies) in the form of tokens (money) that represented labour and its products.

well-being. It was within the temples that the skills of writing, counting and public administration originated, that would make possible the modern nation-state and the global economy.[6] Thus, civilisation was possible because rents were reserved as the material means for the advance of increasingly sophisticated social organisation. This model was the template used on all continents.[7]

The social universe was constructed on the reverence for Earth, and the willingness to abide by rules that secured everyone's right of access to the riches of nature. This combination made possible the deployment of a community's surplus to fund the expansion of social and religious activities. But these civilisations remained experiments in evolution, for they failed to sustain themselves. About 30 civilisations have been buried by the sands of time. Understanding why they ultimately failed may enable our civilisation to avoid (or at least postpone) a similar terminal fate.

Some civilisations disappeared because they abused their primordial contract with nature. By over-exploiting the resources on which they relied, they depleted rather than conserved nature. They failed to align themselves with the reproductive capacity of land. Social life withered, along with the dependent culture. But there was another major reason for the breakdown of civilisations. The violent separation of parts of the population from land proved fatal. Once consolidated into a large-scale process, communities divided by exclusion (as a result of attributing exclusivity to the use of land for the benefit of a minority) were locked into a vertical structure: a hierarchy. Some individuals were designated as superior to others, not on the basis of personal attributes, but because of their exceptional claims on nature, or the surplus product generated by the people who worked on the land. That unnatural arrangement – constructed on a savage infringement of people's natural rights – could only be sustained by building violence into the foundations of society. We do not tolerate such violence on the sporting field (see Box 1:1), but we have come to accept it in our daily lives. And that is because we have

---

6 Hudson (2004).
7 For an account of how rent found its formal institutional expression in Europe in early feudal times, see Maitland (1960: Ch 6).

> **Box 1:1 This Sporting Life**
>
> OTHER social animals can *play*, but sport is unique to humans. It combines cognitive skills in an organised drama that secures efficiency (deployment of human skills) with equality (respect for each participant). Rules create the "level playing field", acknowledging the principle that everyone has the right to be treated as an equal. The referee is the guardian of the rules, the adjudicator who secures equal treatment for everyone.
>
> In the sporting life, the group (team) matters; but so does the individual, who is free to express his or her talents in co-operation with others. Arbitrary advantage or power over others is formally eliminated. For where outstanding skills would lead to a mismatch, arrangements are made to remove the inequality by matching groups according to known achievements. Thus, we end up with "fair play". Both the individual and the group attains the fullest satisfaction through personal effort rather than by diminsishing others.

lost our sense of the unnaturalness of those rules, which generate the pathologies of the capitalist way of life.

The Pathology of Capitalism

CIVILISATIONS deployed policies that made possible enormous advances in the production of wealth. And yet, the monumental achievements of a Rome collapsed under the onslaught of pre-civilised groups armed with primitive technologies. We need to bear such cases in mind as we describe the nature of our civilisation.

The defining characteristics of capitalism are not money, or markets, or energy-mobilising technologies. These existed in pre-capitalist societies. The distinctive characteristic of capitalism is its dualism. Embedded in it are two distinct cultures, each with its social and economic laws and processes. One of them (Culture I: the Predators) depends upon the other (Culture II: the Producers). The Predator culture is parasitic on the Producers. How they were fused, made to co-exist, is central to understanding the institutionalisation of violence as a social process.

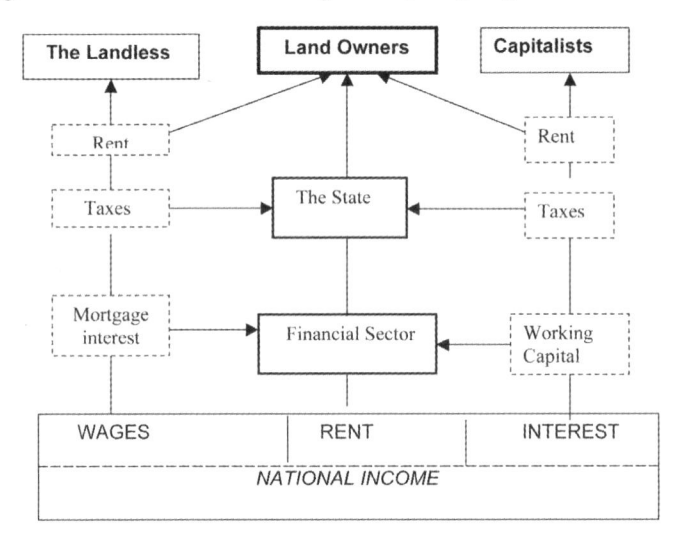

Figure 1:3   The Distribution of Power, Property & Income

```
         The Landless        Land Owners         Capitalists
              ↑                   ↑                   ↑
            Rent              ↗  ↑  ↖              Rent
                             /   |   \
            Taxes  →     The State     ←   Taxes
                             ↓
          Mortgage
          interest  →  Financial Sector  ←  Working
                                              Capital

          WAGES      |      RENT       |      INTEREST
                        NATIONAL INCOME
```

Culture I: The Predators

SHARING Earth was the pre-condition for releasing the latent talents of each individual, to create the fusion of creative energy that secured the intellectual and spiritual leaps into the new (social) universe. But over the past 500 years there evolved an organisational structure that transgressed this primary principle of human evolution.

Figure 1:3 provides an overview of the structure of power and property. Most people are represented as excluded from the riches of Earth. A significant portion of the products of their labour leeches into the hands of the Predators. Rights to the benefits associated with land were – and still are – reserved for a minority. How did this come about, why is it tolerated even in democracies, and what were the consequences for the fabric of the community?

To dominate the homeland space, those who would be lords of the land had to control the ligaments of power, for two reasons. First, they needed to justify exclusive possession of the soil. This entailed the refashioning of law; and, therefore, of the mind-set of the resident population. Second, they had to diminish the share of rent allocated by the community to fund culture. By controlling the power structure, the lords of the land were able to shift the costs of public services onto the wages of Labour, through taxation.

This audacious exercise in social re-engineering entailed intrusion into people's personalities. Recall that the emergence of humans out of nature was made possible by the fusion of ecology with intellect, culture and social relationships, which shaped minds and souls. To de-socialise nature it was necessary to refashion the way people thought and felt. The privatisation of Earth required the transfer of social life away from common people. This entailed the transformation of the egalitarian structure to one based on vertical (hierarchical) relationships. Thus, the Lords of the Land became gatekeepers of people's minds and souls. To accomplish this project, the would-be masters of the social universe had to embody within themselves both the spiritual and secular forms of power.

In modern times, to legitimise the coup against communities (to consolidate the gains from land privatisation), kings necessarily *had* to develop the doctrine of rule by divine right. Henry VIII, for example, orchestrated a change in the spiritual life of England *to grab the sacred lands of the monasteries*. This enabled him to channel the rents into his coffers, and sponsor the reallocation of land to courtiers. The surplus – the rent that sustained the welfare of the community – was secularised. And so, in England, as the agricultural revolution gave way to the industrial revolution, the economy increased its capacity to mobilise energy and expand the methods of producing income. This increase in organisational complexity was facilitated by the new financial architecture, which supported commercial transactions around the globe. To retain their control over this arrangement, land owners had to assume control over the monetary system. This they accomplished by taking control of the national exchequer.

The excluded – the landless – worked without being able to influence how the surplus which they produced was used. Out of their wages they had to sustain their families, pay rents to their land lords and yield an additional portion (taxes) exacted by the state. As rents were placed beyond the reach of the state, taxes assumed increasing importance as the alternative source of revenue. Then, the power to tax labour's income became a further tool for enriching the Predators. For investment in social infrastructure (such as highways) enhanced the productivity of the value-adding economy. But instead of clawing back this added value to fund the capital embodied in the infrastructure, this value was allowed to cascade down into the land market, where it was then pocketed by land owners. Whichever way they turned, the landless labourers – the value-creators – were losers. The state was hijacked to serve the interests of those who preyed on them.

Culture II : The Producers

THROUGH socialisation (being weaned into accepting current practices), people were resigned to this unequal relationship. It was necessary for the Predators to camouflage the impact of Culture I. They succeeded in persuading people that capitalism was a single system, that was intended to *add value* to the wealth of the nation.

Entrepreneurs who created value were disciplined by principles like the obligation to pay for the benefits which they received. The market is the process through which individuals and firms negotiate the terms for the exchange of goods and services. The integrity of that negotiating process depends on the freedom to choose; to enter into contractual arrangements for the exchange of goods and services without coercion. This philosophy contrasted with the dynamics of private land ownership. The rent-taking function is one of pure extraction. Land, after all, is a free gift of nature. Land owners claim a part of the income of producers solely because of the legal documents they possess, which transfer to them the income that others pay for the benefit of using nature's resources.

The two sets of values underpinning *predation* and *production* are diametrically opposed. For the system to function, however, once the predators were within its midst, the two sets of values had to be made to co-exist. This was achieved through the use of military and police power. Violence in various forms was necessary because the owners of land need others to generate the surplus that enables them to live. To achieve this outcome, of living without expending personal energy, predators had to deploy coercion to enforce their will on the excluded.

Following the demise of Soviet communism, no coherent challenge exists to capitalism as a social system. It triumphed, didn't it? Therefore, it must have its virtues. And, indeed, it does. Culture II *adds* value. People *gain* from its operations. The pathological streak in capitalism is located in Culture I, which is camouflaged by those social scientists who fail to embed in their analysis the sordid history that created the violence of deprivation.

And so, violence is concealed within the culture of the host population. No matter how many laws are passed affirming "human rights", no matter how many "safety nets" are constructed by governments, the abusive characteristics of past land grabs remain inscribed in the fabric of communities that were alienated from their natural habitats. Those characteristics include:

- Premature death.[8]
- Poverty of the dispossessed.
- Cultural deprivation, as the surplus income is largely absorbed by land grabbers.
- Social waste, as the appropriators employ brutal techniques to control as much land as possible, even if that means holding their assets in an unused state.
- Environmental devastation.

Thus is the abusive character of capitalism sustained, irrespective of who occupies the positions of power. Personal greed may have inspired the original land grab; but personal sentiments are no longer of importance, because the system sustains itself.

A society divided by the de-socialisation of land cannot evolve a homogenous culture. Attitudes, appearances and behaviour patterns are differentiated by whether one is a rent-taker or a rent-loser. The spatial division of the two groups has such profound consequences that they manifest themselves in differences in personality. The cumulative effect is a culture of *pauperisation*.

---

8 Miller (2003) estimates that about 50,000 people die prematurely, in England and Wales alone, every year, because of the stresses in life that can ultimately be traced back to the tax policies favoured by land owners and their governments.

Chapter 2

The Culture of Pauperisation

The Pathology of Rent Privatisation

RUPTURING people from their habitats – their living communities - is the invasive form of violence that does not recognise boundaries. It is the template that shapes other forms of socially organised violence.

To understand the character of that primary violence, we need to trace the channels through which change is wrought in the lives of the displaced. The conduits of violence are broadly classified in Table 2:1. Column 1 lists the components of the social universe.

Through evolutionary timescales, the progress of the human species was achieved within the framework of biological units that flourished as extended families. These support groups delivered the security that made possible the experiments that enabled individuals to migrate through time and space, to the point where they could create their unique social universe.

Household economies were linked through social structures that regulated group association and behaviour, to secure stability in the use of natural resources.[1] Integrating the economic and social units was the culture, the spiritual, artistic and knowledge base of the community that defines the potential for further progress. These three levels of experience were symbiotically related. The whole edifice was tied together by the allocation of rights of tenure that kept the organic relationships functioning.

---

1 Diamond (1971).

Table 2:1   Conduits of Violence

1 Social Formations	2 The Predators		3 The Excluded
	Primary Intervention	*Mechanisms of Consolidation*	*Some Defensive Reactions*
Household Economy	Displacement of Commoners	Genocide	Organised Crime
Communal Structure	Control through Coercion	Expansionist Territorial Wars	Utopian Escapism
Culture	Appropriation of Aesthetics and Technology	Monopoly of Communications	Religious Fundamentalism

Strategies employed by those who appropriate the land of others are listed in column 2. As the first step, households clustered in village communities were displaced, a brutal physical separation of people and Earth where, before, the primary ethic was the sharing of land in common.[2] The social universe was abruptly destroyed once rights of access were terminated.[3]

Abstracting from the complexities of tenure, we can say that there were two broad formulas for using land. Each household held parcels which were hereditary. An individual's membership of the household defined the right of access. With social evolution, and the clustering of households into village communities, land was held that could be used in common by these household units. Rights of access were the membrane of the biological, kinship-based households, which united in the village framework to increase productivity and the quality of life. Rights to land bound people together, securing their future through their association with the landscape.[4]

To overturn this arrangement, land-grabbers had to manipulate the institutions that make and enforce laws. But to sustain their control in perpetuity, they had to seize control of culture. The religious and aesthetic life of the population had to be appropriated and re-shaped, if only to eliminate competing sources of authority. In essence, the

---

2 Vinogradoff (1968), Pollock and Maitland (1968).
3 Peake (1922). Coulton (1925), Hogue (1986).
4 Maitland (1908), Stephenson (1954).

cultural framework of life in its totality had to be privatised for the benefit of a privileged minority. This was achieved by the private consumption of the economic surplus that was generated by people who were tied as tenants to the land. The landless were excluded from participation in the creative activities that defined humans as distinct from other primates. They were regressively dehumanised.

Once communities were restructured along dysfunctional lines, the logic of the new structure of power and income distribution propelled the elites along a distinctive path. They developed an appetite for consumption unchecked by any corresponding obligation to labour. That appetite was insatiable. So to sustain it, they had to continuously expand their sphere of territorial influence. Spatial expansion necessitated wars and other forms of violence. On occasion, that entailed not the mere displacement or enslavement of people, but wholesale destruction (genocide). With the expansion of territorial control, culture had to be further modified to incorporate cost-effective technologies of supervision over the population that was alienated from the land. This included censoring the language of communication, meaning the control over people's minds.

Violence, however, begets violence. And so, the excluded are driven to defensive strategies. Column 3 identifies some of the categories of reaction. Through their households, dispossessed families may organise themselves into criminal fraternities. These include the Mafia "families" that emerged out of the margins of the Italian peninsula. For others, appeal to mass mobilisation of violence is attractive. Karl Marx's call to class warfare illustrates how socially organised violence may be expressed in the language of revolution. One outcome is the channelling of people away from the source of their problem towards utopianism. And within the chinks in the armour of a perverted culture – in which poverty is endemic – people may escape into political extremism or religious fundamentalism. One consequence is the perversion of politics or religion to legitimise the resort to violence.

Thus, beginning with the act of depriving people of their right of access to Earth, we may trace the replication of violence through to the impacts on victims. They suffer material and spiritual deprivation, subordinated to the organising principle of such a society: the deployment of violence to control people, regulating the way that they behave, think and feel.

This contrasts with what happens in communities in which natural rights to land and biological security are respected. People are guided through the life cycle by participating in groups defined by age, by gender and by social roles (spiritual or secular) which enable their communities to flourish. Rituals and values facilitated the individual's needs; unifying members of the group, integrating them into an organically healthy association. That homogeneity disintegrates when a population is divided by the privatisation of the surplus product. Two kinds of distinct association emerge.

At the top of the hierarchy of power are the arrangements defined in the interest of land appropriators. These range from rituals (such as those associated with the feudal doctrine of chivalry), to country sports such as fox hunting, to the gentlemen's clubs that cluster around the urban centres of political power. These institutions are designed as mechanisms of exclusion. They are intended to disable others. Binding that kind of society, we find institutions such as the professional armies that are used to drill people into compliance (as they are mobilised to defend the privileges of the elites), and folk institutions of the "lower orders". The one constant element in this mélange of pain is that people are systematically deprived of the freedom to realise their potential.

The psychology of the population corresponds to the bifurcation of power. Lords of the land display attitudes of superiority; they command, after all, the means for creating the social universe. The landless adopt postures of compliance. Theirs is a life of suppressed feelings and intellect, the stunted formation of personality. This violence of the psyche finds its public expression in the rituals of deference to one's "betters". Fear is the glue that holds together such communities, fear of others and of the future. The atrophy of cultural and psychological potential expresses itself in the *pauperisation* of society. Its essence is the corruption of the freedom that is needed to enjoy the life of one's choosing within a community that is not distorted by the monopolisation of land (see Box 2:1).

> **Box 2:1 "Chains of the Ghosts of the Past"**
>
> IN JUNE 2008, islanders who were ejected from their homelands in the Indian Ocean sought justice in Britain's highest court. Turfed off the Chagos Islands to make way for a US base, the islanders sought redress by claiming the right to return.
>
> About 2,000 of them from Diego Garcia and surrounding islands were expelled between 1965 and 1973 and resettled on Mauritius. Pauperisation began with the resort to alcoholism, drugs and prostitution.
>
> Britain's Foreign Office resisted their right to return, even though that right was recognised by the High Court. The Foreign Office fought their case all the way to the House of Lords. The islanders were tied to what the High Court judges called "the chains of the ghosts of the past" – the colonial deeds of land dispossession that saw human rights brushed aside in favour of the geo-politics of colonial empires.
>
> In October 2008, the Law Lords ruled that the British government was not acting unlawfully in preventing the islanders returning to their ancestral homes. The islanders, pronounced the Law Lords, had received fair compensation.
>
> No amount of monetary compensation can offset the psycho-social damage caused when people are ruptured from their homeland.

The Corruption of Power

WHEN rent was privatised, coveted for exclusively self-centred purposes, the vitality of society ebbed away. Culture, as the fabric of the evolutionary process, was corrupted. For when Earth was deprived of its social significance, humanity itself was deformed, beginning with the spiritual life.

The privatisation of rent necessarily entailed the transfer of power from the deities to mortal men. Henry VIII, for example, confused his venal needs with his social function. To privatise the lands of England it was necessary to disengage those life-sustaining acres from the spiritual function vested in them by the people. Thus, Henry engineered a two-stage re-sculpturing of the social landscape. He expropriated the lands of the monasteries, to enrich himself and his courtiers; and in doing so, he was able to vest in himself the power of God – literally, the power of life and death. The doctrine of the divine right of kings to rule was inextricably bound up with the de-socialisation of land.

The impact stemming from the secularisation of Earth may be traced in the transformation of the laws of tenure. Primogeniture, for example, was invented to secure monopolistic domination over the land through time. Estates were inherited by the eldest son.[5] This enabled land owning families to preserve their identities and memories as these were embodied in estates. Their history was conserved and celebrated in opulent paintings and leather-bound chronicles. Their tenants suffered a transient existence on the nether regions of the landscape, their rudimentary lives unchronicled, reliant on the fleeting memories of the living. The community is pauperised, materially, spiritually and psychologically. But the lords of the land are also victimised, for their humanity is starved of the accomplishments that would otherwise be achieved by people in free communion.

- *Outcasts* are deprived of the self esteem that is integrally related to participation as full members of the community.
- *Rent-takers* are morally impoverished as they dissipate creative energy in destructive deeds to preserve their privileges.

Everyone loses. Personalities are suffused in the culture of deprivation. Social, spiritual and intellectual life is starved of the resources needed to give expression to the human potential. The dispossessed struggle for their biological subsistence while those who possess the land segregate themselves in strongholds, deprived of their share of the riches that would otherwise flow from the unimpeded association between people.

This is a social arrangement of violence in its purest form. Humanity is dissipated to satisfy the gluttony of the few. Land owners are necessarily de-humanised, so that they may more efficiently continue to abuse the rights of others. And their victims come to accept their de-sensitised state as a defence mechanism, the psychological armour needed to survive the systematic abuse inflicted on them. With time, people assume this state of affairs to be natural.

---

5 Milsom (1981: Ch.8).

And yet, we are haunted by the harmonies of the past when we trace, inscribed in the landscape, what anthropologists call "survivals".

Before the de-socialisation of land, settlements were sympathetically integrated into their habitats. Spatial relationships expressed meanings that constituted the social universe, designed to articulate the cosmic sweep of the human mind. Villages in the Basque region that straddles the borders of Spain and France, for example, project meanings beyond the earthly status of their inhabitants.

> Not only did the Basques inhabit an organised spatial universe with permanent farms and roads of the living and roads of the dead connected to the church and cemetery, but they also symbolised these relations on the church floor and in their pattern of mourning the dead… the 'village of the living' thus became collectively responsible for the welfare of the 'village of the dead,' being united by the geographic layout of the village itself. The village landscape was both a setting for daily activity and a sacred geography summing up the relation between the living and the dead and all the people's hope for salvation.[6]

People nurtured into such communities revered nature and were constrained from abusing their habitats. This configuration between people and the land, the present and the future, the living and the dead, may be contrasted with the practices employed in settlements embedded in a culture that is pathologically distorted by rent privatisation, in which land is deprived of its sacred value.

Settlers in the New World, in the main, had been brutally displaced from their birthright access to land in Europe. Bringing with them the indoctrination that sustained those European countries, they reshaped the landscape of America on the basis of an ethic that treated nature as savage, which had to be tamed. Nature was not a partner in the creative challenge to enrich the social universe. She had to be subordinated. This attitude found its spatial expression in the straight lines of the

---

6 Greenwood and Stini (1977: 147).

layout of settlements. Overriding the contours of the landscape, the settlers were not driven by doctrines of economic efficiency, or the evolutionary quest for a symbiotic relationship with the landscape. They were not concerned with *conservation*. Their motivation was land speculation, the commodification of nature, a quick way to make money out of the labours of others.

- Land was wasted. Settlers were forced to leapfrog the sites hoarded by real estate speculators who chose to quarantine their land whilst awaiting higher capital gains from the sale at some indeterminate time in the future.
- Capital was wasted. Over-investment in shared services (highways, utilities, and so on) across larger spaces, was necessary to accommodate the urban sprawl induced by land speculation.

These economic practices are not acknowledged as forms of systemic violence, but they are violence in action, depriving people of their liberties and incomes to assuage the avarice of land speculators.

Today, we live with the growing realisation that the damage inflicted on our habitats is likely to exact a terrible price. Desperately poor people exploit nature for short-term survival, even though they may be aware that such ruinous deeds will deprive them of resources in the future. Forests in the Himalayas, for example, are felled for fuel by families who, forced on to the margins of existence, are prevented from meeting their energy needs by using sustainable methods. By such actions they wash away the top soils downstream, that others need to grow food. Such misguided behaviour is driven by the norms of a pauperised culture.

Nature versus Nurture

AT THE beginning of the third millennium, the global community of nations was in an extreme state of disarray. The economic base of most communities buckled. Property markets fell off a precipice as land prices peaked in 2007.[7] Suddenly, the doctrines on which governments based

---

7 Harrison (2005).

their policies were discredited (these included the assumptions that markets are efficient, and economies are self-correcting mechanisms). Shell-shocked economists turned to exotic ways of trying to decipher why financial markets had seized up. Psychology offered apparently rigorous approaches to the origins of economic disorder. Neuroscience – studying people's brains – became fashionable.[8]

The link between the collapse of the economic structure, and the prospect of an intensification of violence, became an increasingly threatening prospect as governments struggled to keep their banking sectors afloat; which suggests that there was more at work than media commentators liked to admit (see Box 2:2).

Box 2:2 From Land Speculation to Systemic violence

AS THE global economy crashed into its worst crisis since the Great Depression of the 1930s, analysts became aware of the mounting risks of social unrest. The Economist Intelligence Unit (EIU) found that, of the 165 countries it reviewed in its Political Instability Index (based on 15 social, political and economic indicators), 95 countries were "in the very high risk or high risk group".[1]

What was provoking the risk of organized violence among people who were losing jobs and their homes? My forecasts, published in 1997 and 2005, predicted that the loss of employment would be due to land speculation, which drove the price of residential property to unaffordable levels.[2] Perusal of the media reveals the threads that link the social malaise in property rights to land.

- In London, local authorities became alarmed because they were legally forced to reveal the addresses of vacant properties to squatters. Empty properties in Britain mounted to 1m as homes were repossessed by mortgage lenders.[3]
- Owners of second homes in idyllic villages became targets for vandalism as the rural housing crisis intensified, with people displaced by the unaffordable price of the dwellings in their communities.[4]

1 EIU (2009: 19-20). 2 Harrison (1997, 2005). 3 Allen (2009). 4 Walker (2009).

---

8 Niehoff (1999), Taylor (2009).

But these new approaches to understanding the economic crisis place responsibility for disorder on the individual, rather than the rules that structure society. Rationalisations, such as "it's human nature", suit the rent-seekers. They distract attention from the systemic roots of violence.

To break down the complex circumstances surrounding individual deeds, we need to recognise that the causes of violence may be located along a continuum. In fact, there are several continuums. One records the types of violence. These range from the weakest forms (for example, verbal abuse by children in the playground) to the most extreme acts of brutality that result in the deaths of millions.

Figure 2:1 provides a schematic framework that accommodates competing theories. On it we can locate behaviour ranging from perverse actions that are the sole responsibility of the perpetrator, to the premeditated acts that stem from the wilful ordinances of the state (such as Nazi Germany's Holocaust and Stalin's purges in Soviet Russia).

The horizontal axis measures the contribution of institutions and laws to violence. These range from the weakest forms (inhibiting people from working, for example, by taxing their labour) to the suborning of people into obedience so that they follow orders to kill.

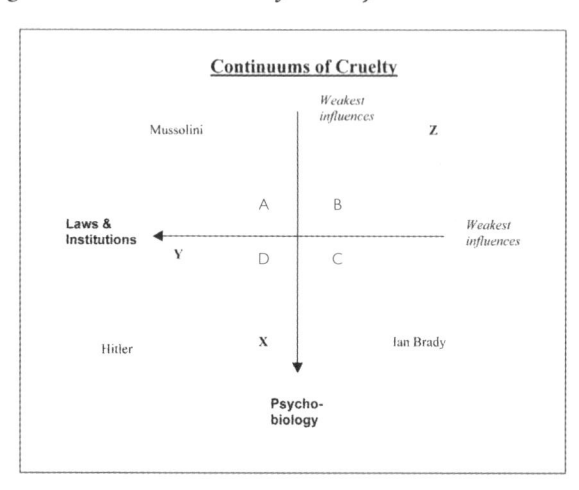

Figure 2:1 Continuums of Cruelty

Continuums of Cruelty

- Mussolini (upper left)
- Z (upper right, near *Weakest influences*)
- A, B (middle upper quadrants)
- Laws & Institutions ← Y
- D, C (middle lower quadrants)
- *Weakest influences* (right)
- Hitler (lower left)
- X (lower middle)
- Ian Brady (lower right)
- Psycho-biology (bottom)

The vertical axis measures personal propensities as revealed in psychological profiles. These range from the weakest fantasies about harming others (an angry person declaring: "I would kill him if I could get hold of him") to the most cold-hearted intention to brutalise and kill without qualm.

For illustrative purposes, I place the deeds represented by Mussolini at the north-west corner of quadrant A. We cannot account for such behaviour in terms of personal psychological failing. As I explain in Chapter 9, his murderous behaviour is made intelligible in terms of the logic of a specific institutional framework. Living patterns in Italy at the time fostered the political action that led to the appropriation of territories in Africa. There, the forcible appropriation of other people's land could only be executed through the application of state violence (see Box 2:3).

Some individuals behave cruelly with no apparent social pressure to account for their actions. Ian Brady is an example. He did not enjoy a secure home and full parental nurturing. He was raised in a tough neighbourhood of Glasgow, which did not give him the best start in life. Many other children were raised under similar circumstances, but they did not turn into serial killers of children. During 18 hours of intense discussions with him in his prison cell, I was offered a distressing insight into a psychology that formed the basis of his sadistic murder of five children.[9] I could not attribute his deeds to social conditions. I locate Brady in the south-east corner of quadrant C, not least because he made no attempt to blame society for his behaviour.

Some individuals would be located in quadrant D. This would include psychologically damaged people whose personal proclivities sent them in search of a perverse social cause within which to express their violent inclinations (how many dictators would fit this profile?). They would be placed (for example) close to point [x], rather than point [y], since that would be using the social context more as an excuse for cruelty, rather than as the cause of their behaviour.

---

9 Harrison (1986).

> **Box 2:3 Mussolini's Mental Health**
>
> THE state of mind of the Italian Marxist who invented Fascism was affirmed by Sigmund Freud, who signed a copy of a book he co-authored with Albert Einstein, inscribed: "To Benito Mussolini, from an old man who greets in the Ruler, the Hero of Culture".[1]
>
> Hitler's mental health, on the other hand, may be inferred from the project which he incubated at an early age. French philosopher Michel Foucault summarised the elements of his megalomaniacal fantasy in terms of achieving the purity of the German race through death and, if necessary, collective suicide.[2] This suggests that Hitler should be located in the extreme corner of quadrant D in Fig. 2:1.
>
> 1 Goldberg (2007: 27).   2 Foucault (2003:257).

Ideally, we would like to live in communities with people located near to point [z]. Here, there is little or no personal or social pressure to behave violently. But that is a utopian world – or is it?

That humans are capable of wickedness beyond that of any other species cannot be contested. Our capacity for imagination makes those deeds possible. But humans are also capable of selfless acts. Our quest, then, is the search for the combination of laws and institutions that nurture goodness rather than violence. To remind ourselves that the constitution for a peaceful society can be constructed, we will examine the roots of a modern nation that has chosen to dismantle its standing army, that singular symbol of organised violence.

CHAPTER 3
THE SOCIO-ECOLOGY OF PEACE: COSTA RICA

A FAILED state is popularly conceived as one that exports terrorism to New York, London or Madrid. But as we shall discover, the problem of the failed state is more complex and needs closer scrutiny if we are to lance the festering influences within the global body politic which incubate the conditions that lead to the making of suicide bombers.

What does a successful nation-state look like? It is one where people are locally integrated into their communities while relating harmoniously to their chosen form of governance. So far, this statement tells us little. We need to confront one of the most challenging issues, namely, the attitude of the individual to the political system as mediated by taxation. A successful state may be defined as a non-violent one in which the individual freely defrays the costs of public services without the need for coercion. Joseph Schumpeter drew attention to this reality in his *History of Economic Analysis*.

> Since nothing shows so clearly the character of a society and of a civilisation as does the fiscal policy that its political sector adopts, we shall expect current and counter-current to show particularly clearly in this field. They do.[1]

---
1 Schumpeter (1954: 769).

Any state that needs to apply force to raise revenue is on the road to failure. Taxation assumes a violent form to the degree that people cease to regard payments as voluntary contributions to the common good. Historically, this happened as the character of the revenue system shifted away from the earliest method, of paying for the use of resources that were regarded as common property, to levies on earned incomes and on property. The collateral effect of the transformation in the character of taxation was (a) the erosion of control over territory, and (b) the need to raise revenue by deploying sub-optimum methods.

The emergence of the modern state was executed on the back of the land grabbing project by post-feudal aristocratic elites. This dictated the need for coercion at the outset. The way in which that state may lose control is illustrated by the rise in competing centres of power which have acquired the means of coercion. Thus, organised crime consists of gangs that levy revenue that would normally – in a healthy state – flow into the exchequer of the formal state. The Mafia demand protection money from businesses: this is a charge on location exacted by the shadow state. But organised crime can flourish only when the formal state has lost some of its legitimacy, and is therefore incapable of providing protection for the people. This breakdown in the relationship between the state and the people arises where the agents of the state abuse power (see Chapter 8).

Mussolini tried to eliminate the Mafia. Ultimately, he failed because he employed the policies (grabbing other people's land) which were the reasons why organised crime emerged in Italy in the first place. His attempt to solve contemporary economic problems (such as the unemployment of the depression years of the 1930s) was founded on principles that ruptured communities at their foundations. So no matter how much counter violence he applied, Italy could not expunge the conditions that nurtured the need (in a part of its population) for the security afforded by the shadow state.

Figure 3:1 offers a comparison of two measures which register the degree of loss of control over territory. The horizontal axis measures the intensity of coercion. The vertical axis represents the inability of

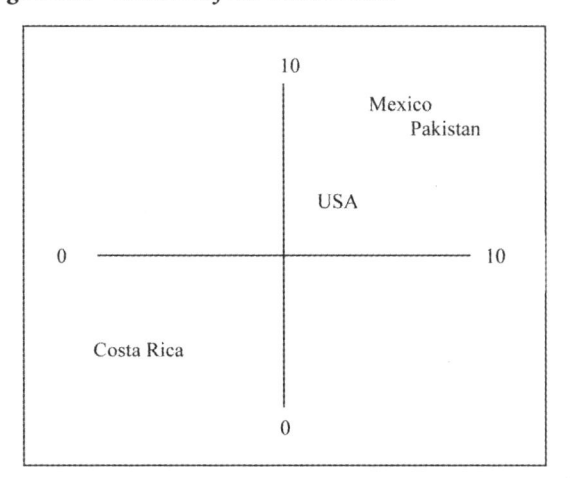

Figure 3:1   Metrics of the Failed State

```
                         10
                              Mexico
                              Pakistan

                         USA
  0 ─────────────────────┼───────────── 10

          Costa Rica

                          0
```

the formal state to control its territory; and, especially, control over its sources of public revenue.

In the northeast quadrant we locate two notorious cases: Mexico, where the government is in a perpetual war with narco trafficking gangs across its territory, and Pakistan, which is at war with religious fundamentalist who seek to use politics to control the spiritual life of the resident population. The USA is placed just inside this quadrant to draw attention to the fact that what is generally portrayed as a stable polity is marred by characteristics of the failed state. One indicator is the scale of the imprisonment of a mainly African American population for their extra-legal economic activities.

In the southwest quadrant we place Costa Rica, where the resort to coercion is severely limited. This country has formally abandoned the need for an army as a regulatory tool of the state. How this happened is a case study in the social ecology of building a nation on the principles of peace and prosperity.

Rural Democracy

COSTA RICA is not typical of countries in Latin America. There were few rich pickings to attract the *conquistadors*. Just land – vast stretches of virgin soil and lush vegetation. No people to enslave in the 18th century, no gold to dig out in the 19th century, no petroleum to extract in the 20th century. So Costa Rica became a haven of relative peace and prosperity in the heart of central America's Zone of Violence. The facts are not contested, but their interpretation is challenged.

Costa Ricans depended on subsistence farming (which removed the risk of class cleavages). Colonial society was bucolic and egalitarian, grounded in self-sufficient but small and medium-sized family farms. Costa Ricans promote this history as the reality of their past, a rural democracy, but it has been questioned.[2]

Table 3:1 contrasts Costa Rica's *per capita* income and growth rate with her four neighbours. Unlike Nicaragua and Honduras, Costa Rica does not have seams of gold in her hills. Unlike Guatemala, Costa Rica cannot cash-in on the global thirst for petroleum. And yet, she is able to generate a *per capita* income more than double the size of the countries surrounding her borders. This astonishing difference cannot be explained in terms of the tax rates. All five countries have similar top income and corporate tax rates at 25% or 30%.

Costa Rica invests more in infrastructure and the welfare of citizens than her neighbours. Furthermore, she retains a *civil* security force that is half or a third the size of the armies of her neighbours. Consequently, almost one-third of the national budget is devoted to primary and secondary education. How do we account for this remarkable difference?

Table 3:1   The Zone of Violence (some Vital Statistics, 2005)

	GDP (Purchasing Power Parity) Per capita: $	Growth Rate: % (2005)	Population (millions)	Government Expenditure as % of GDP
Costa Rica	10,180	5.9	4.3	20.5
Nicaragua	3,674	4.0	5.1	27.3
El Salvador	5,254	2.8	6.9	18.6
Honduras	3,430	4.1	7.2	24.1
Guatemala	4,568	3.2	12.6	11.7

Source: *2007 Index of Economic Freedom*, Washington DC: The Heritage Foundation, 2008.

---

2   Wilson (1998: 12).

One explanation is that the whiteness of the population facilitated the shift to democracy. This is dismissed as a notion "which is as false as it is racist".[3] The ethnic homogeneity of Costa Rica is notable. Charles Ameringer suggests that "it is more reasonable to affirm that where you don't have a system based upon the domination of one race or culture by another", you get social cohesion and the absence of the class divisions that mar the other isthmus territories. This is not a plausible response, however. Domination of one group by another was (and is) apparent even in ethnically homogeneous societies, such as those in central and southern Europe.

Given their common colonial heritage, and close proximity, why did the other four countries suffer civil conflicts and economic exploitation? Why did Costa Rica remain largely immune from the civil strife that tore apart her neighbours in the last half of the 20th century? Could it be that the circumstances which resulted in ethnic homogeneity also disposed the people of this territory to the conditions that generated higher levels of income, and a stable civil society?

> It is a cliché that there are more school teachers than soldiers in Costa Rica, but it is one founded in reality. Patriotic holidays are observed with parades by school children, rather than by reviews of troops and military hardware.[4]

While other developing countries spend fortunes on equipping their military forces – with money borrowed from Western banks, incurring debts from which they are unable to escape – Costa Rica struck out on a unique path of social development.

The seminal event was the election of February 1948. The governing party was defeated, but refused to accept the verdict of the polls. It claimed that there had been fraud, and the election was declared invalid. Civil war broke out, and within two months the governing party, which was backed by the army against the uprising of the *civil* population, was defeated. Power was transferred to Don José Figueres

---

3 Ameringer (1982: 3).
4 Ameringer (1982:)2.

Ferrer, who became president of the Junta. Within seven months he abolished the army, whose barracks was converted into a museum. From then on, Costa Rica became an unarmed democracy, an oasis of peace in a region of armed-to-the-teeth dictatorships of both the Left and of the Right.

Land & Freedom

FOLLOWING the abolition of the military, Costa Rica embarked on a course that was unique in the neo-colonial world. Incomes immediately started to equalise, with those in the bottom half moving up the scale (Table 3:2). People in the top income bracket became fewer in number as the middle class expanded in response to changes that included the increase in minimum wages, and comprehensive free health care insurance. One author called this outcome "the peculiar brand of elitist democracy functioning in this country".[5]

Attempts were made to persuade Costa Rica to re-militarise itself, or at least to abandon its neutral stance. It refused, persisting with the philosophy that was eloquently reaffirmed by Luis Alberto Monge (president from 1982 to 1986) in these terms:

> Neutrality must be unarmed; we disarmed unilaterally. There is no such thing as a military solution. We have no wish to create an army; we have no money to buy weapons. We remain convinced – as we have been over 35 years since

Table 3:2   Relative Changes in Costa Rican Income Distribution: 1964-1973

Percent of Population	Percent of Family Income 1963	1973
Lowest 20%	6.0	5.4
Next 60%	34.0	44.0
Next 10%	14.0	16.2
Highest 10%	46.0	34.4
	100	100

Source: Victor Hugo Céspedes, *Costa Rica: La Distribución Del Ingreso Y LEL Consumo de Algunos Alimentos*, San José: IECES. University of Costa Rica, 1972, p. 41.

---

5 Guess (1979: 24).

we disbanded our armed forces – that poor countries do not have resources for education and an army. We choose education, health and the welfare of our people. There is no alternative, we do not have the resources for both these and an army. We intend to maintain our position.[6]

Under the constitution of 1949, internal authority is enforced by a civil guard. Critics have suggested that Costa Rica relied on the goodwill of other countries, and especially the USA, for protection. But in this, it is no different from European countries that sheltered under the NATO umbrella, the mainstay of which is the USA.

What was it about the history of this territory that made it possible for a nation to renounce militarism? The seeds were sown in the early decades following its discovery by Christopher Columbus in 1502. This was a land that failed to attract the *conquistadors*. Those who did settle here, basing themselves in the Central Valley, were unable to wage war against the indigenous population, which was remotely located in inaccessible regions. Furthermore, in 1542, laws were passed which ordained that the Indians were to be treated as the vassals of the King of Spain. This meant they could not be converted into slaves nor forced to labour.

Thus, absent from Costa Rica was the institutionalised form of labour conflict that was characteristic of the *hacienda* estate, the favoured model of land tenure elsewhere in Latin America. Relationships were based on mutual interest. Costa Rica enjoyed what a World Bank study called a social contract, which reflected the inter-dependence between those who held extensive units of land (especially in the north-west region of Guanacaste), and seasonal workers. High wages were paid, thanks to "the relative scarcity of labour, the relative abundance of land, and the prevailing system of small property holdings".[7]

From the start of its settlement by Spaniards early in the 16th century through to the introduction of coffee as a cash crop in the middle of the 19th century, farming was based on small scale subsistence holdings.

---

6 Bird (1984: 185).
7 World Bank (1993: 69).

Coffee increased the nation's income and for the first time generated a substantial rental surplus. But because of the independence of all citizens – a freedom based on ready access to land – the introduction of a cash crop and the pursuit of profit did not lead to the exploitation that is characteristic of what passes for the typical capitalist economy. Instead, there emerged an implicit contract that reflected what the World Bank called "a delicate equilibrium". Reciprocity was the principle that enabled the various economic groups to relate to each other. Firms that combined farming, processing and exporting did not exercise power over the small and medium-sized proprietorships based on family labour. "In exchange for stability, protection, and employment, the *campesino* provided loyalty, labour, his production surpluses, and a degree of political subordination."[8]

This relative prosperity was determined by the fact that settlers had to work the land themselves if they wanted to live off it. They could not be *conquistadors*.

> They had to become *campesinos* instead, small farmers who got their hands and boots dirty subsisting on their own land. In the next century, far to the north, Thomas Jefferson would talk and dream about how the independent landowner, the small farmer, could become the backbone and ballast of true democracy. In Costa Rica, midwifed by poverty, geography, and luck, a form of Jeffersonian democracy was already being born.[9]

Because land was available, settlers were free to work for themselves. As a result, "employees were in demand, so they were paid wages and often could choose for whom to work".[10] Landowners had to negotiate deals that were acceptable to the people who agreed to work for them rather than for themselves on their own land (Table 3:3). This would have a striking impact on both the culture and the collective consciousness of the population.

---

8 Vega Carballo, (1982: 25).
9 Rolbein (1989: 23).
10 Rolbein (1989: 23).

Table 3:3   Real Working-class Wage Indices, Central American Countries (1973=100)

	Costa Rica	El Salvador	Guatemala	Honduras	Nicaragua
1963	80	90	-	-	92
1973	100	100	100	100	100
1983	102	60	85	92	49
1993	134	35	69	49	2[1]

1 Hyperinflation and collapse of Nicaragua's exchange rate in the late 1980s rendered the wage index functionally meaningless.
Source: John A. Booth and Thomas W. Walker, *Understanding Central America*, Boulder: Westview Press, 1989, Appendix Table IV.

[T]he rural population was free to move, which led the owners of *fincas* to compete for workers and to treat them well. The new coffee *finca* arose under circumstances quite different from those of the Hispanic *latifundia* [large landed estate]…The patron was not an absentee landlord. He attended the peasants' fiestas, and they his, and the peasants danced with the wife of the patron.[11]

Costa Rica evolved to prove that it was possible to achieve quality of life standards equal to those of industrialised countries, despite its relatively lower income.

The indicators in Table 3:4 reveal that, on a *per capita* income of a little more than a quarter of the income of industrialised countries, Costa Rica's citizens enjoy higher life expectancy than in the industrialised countries, and a lower infant mortality rate compared to her neighbours in Central America. This challenges the conventional wisdom of economists and policy-makers, that to raise living standards it is necessary to generate high rates of growth on the principles advocated by "the Washington Consensus".[12] Costa Rica does enjoy the benefits of "a unique model of social development",[13] *not* by growing faster, but by reforming the approach to social development. The key to Costa Rica's development is the relationship between the population and its

11 Ameringer (1982: 3).
12 Harrison (2008).
13 Garnier et al (1997: 359).

Table 3:4   Human development in Costa Rica and Other Countries (1992)

Indicator	Costa Rica	Rest of central America	Industrialised Countries
Life Expectancy at birth (years)	76.0	64.8	74.5
Infant Mortality (per '000 live births)	14	52	13
Mortality – under age 5 (per'000 live births)	16	69	15
Per Capita real GDP (PPA in dollars)	5,100	2,545	19,000

Source: Garnier *et al* (1997: 357, Table 12:2).

natural habitat. Despite the gaps in incomes, people are not divided by class attitudes and behaviour based on crushing the majority into a state of dependency.

> In the Costa Rican countryside, it was possible for economic inequality to co-exist with high levels of cultural and social equality, which can be illustrated by the fact that the children of the agricultural labourers went to the same schools and to the same health clinics as a majority of the children of the owners of the farms on which their fathers worked.[14]

In Costa Rica, it was *not* necessary to own land to enjoy a quality of life comparable to the landowners. This was achieved because of the social history of settlement in this region, and because of the ambitious programme for distributing land to landless rural families in 1962. This, coupled with the elimination of the financial burden of an army, made it possible to target social spending on low income families without sacrificing the welfare of the middle class.

Land, Labour & Capital

WE get a sense of the way the demilitarised state supported its citizens by comparing the living standards of employees in Costa Rica with how their neighbours fared in Guatemala and Honduras. Table 3:5 compares the remuneration of employees of the American owned

---

14 Garnier et al (1997: 360).

Table 3:5   United Fruit Company, Wages ($ equivalents) paid to agricultural labourers in 1967: $

	Legal Minimum per Day	Average Basic Wage	Average Daily Wage including fringe benefits
Guatemala	-	2.73	3.74
Honduras	-	3.38	4.05
Costa Rica	2.42	4.04	5.00

Source: Villanueva (1969: 67).

United Fruit Company, which then exercised a near monopoly over the banana trade in Central America.

Underpinning wages with a legal minimum did not prejudice the plantation workers in Costa Rica. United Fruit, during the 1960s, invested more capital in its operations in that country than in Guatemala or Honduras. The combination of the higher wage and capital formation generated higher labour productivity in Costa Rica than in the other two countries.[15] Paying higher wages did not prevent a high rate of profit on its investments. United Fruit paid, on average, 25% of its profits to Central American governments, transferring the difference to its American shareholders.

The difference in the incomes of employees could not be explained by differential bargaining power in Costa Rica, because United Fruit faced similar labour union conditions in all three countries.[16] The major difference lay in the fact that *Costa Rica's workers had greater opportunities to withdraw their labour to work for themselves on land that was more freely available in their country than in neighbouring territories.*

An illuminating insight into the role of land in United Fruit's operations is revealed by the fact that its Honduras division made a return of almost double what it was extracting out of Costa Rica. One explanation emerged in the US District Court of Louisiana, when the company was forced to divest itself of assets because it had engaged

---

15   Villaneuva (1969: pp. 63, 65).
16   Villanueva (1969: p. 69).

in "unlawful restraints and monopolies".[17] The company was accused of using its ownership of land and of railways to increase its profits above competitive levels. In relation to Guatemala, it had sold banana plantations with covenants that prevented the land from being used again to grow bananas. This limited the competition it faced, to the benefit of the rate of return on its investments in that country.

The Prize of Peace

BUT the case of Costa Rica is not all good news. We shall see how, despite its policy of demilitarisation, that country could have been even more successful. The United Fruit Company exercised – legally – influence over public policy that restrained trade and people's freedoms in a way that was not exposed in a US Federal Court. That power was a variant of the violence which inhibited Costa Rica from achieving the full potential of a successful – free – state.

The prize of peace is enormous. The costs of state (and quasi-state) sponsored violence are mind-boggling. The economic benefit of peace in 2007, for example (if peace could have been imposed), is estimated at $7.2 trillion. Over a 10-year period, the total peace dividend would have been US$72 trillion.[18] Surely that's sufficient additional revenue to make it possible to pension off the war mongers? But this measure is a small part of the benefit. For organised violence is not confined to set-piece battles between opposing armies. It also comes in other forms, all of which exact a terrible human and material price.

Nevertheless, the prize for embedding peace in social relations, *even when the benefits are measured within communities that labour under sub-optimal policies*, are astonishing. Attempts have been made to quantify those benefits, as reported by Paul Collier, the Director for the Centre for the Study of African Economies at Oxford University. The cost of a typical civil war in a poor country is put at about $64bn. In Africa alone, there have been over 200 coup attempts in the past 30 years, some of which resulted in genocide. Those conflicts are

---

17 USA vs Untied Fruit Company, Civil Action No. 4560, US District Court, Eastern District of Louisiana, February 4, 1958.
18 Economists for Peace & Security, wwwepsusa.org, cited in Institute for Economics and Peace (2009: 30).

contests over the rents of natural resources such as "blood diamonds" in Sierra Leone. Around 11% of foreign aid intended to "develop" these countries ends up in paying for the armaments imported from Western manufacturers.

> Hence, there is a grim interconnection between aid, coups, military spending, and civil war. Military spending in countries where civil war has broken out is typically increased by 1.8% of GDP.[19]

According to Nicole and Mark Crane, "if there were no terrorism incidents in 2002, world GDP would have been US$3.6 trillion higher than it was in that year".[20] This is a loss of wealth equal to 7-9% of world GDP. This cost will rise as disaffected groups secure dirty bombs, nuclear and chemical weapons and other tools of mass destruction.

The incentive to uncover the secret of peace is enormous. The peace code is buried in the rules that regulate our relationship with nature.

---

19   Collier (2007: 223-224).
20   Crane and Crane (2005), cited in Linotte (2007: 268).

Part 2

The Social Pathology of Land Grabs

Few have been more marginalized and ignored by Washington for as long as Native Americans – our First Americans. We know the history that we share. It's a history marked by violence and disease and deprivation. Treaties were violated. Promises were broken. You were told your lands, your religion, your cultures, your languages, were not yours to keep. And that's a history that we've got to acknowledge if we are to move forward. – Barack Obama

CHAPTER 4

COLONIALISM & THE CORRUPTION OF PEOPLE POWER

IN the mid-19th century, children were taught to celebrate the killing or displacement of people from their land. English historian Edward Freeman, for example, championed the Anglo-Saxon campaign to eliminate rivals, the Romano-Britons, the ancestors of the Welsh. He wrote that "it has turned out much better in the end that our forefathers did thus kill or drive out nearly all the people whom they found in the land…[since otherwise] I cannot think that we should ever have been so great and free a people as we have been for many ages".[1] But it was also in the 19th century that sociologist Herbert Spencer (1820-1903) noted in the first edition of *Social Statics* that

> an exclusive possession of the soil necessitates an infringement of the law of equal freedom. For, men who cannot "live and move and have their being" without the leave of others, cannot be equally free with those others. [2]

The colonisation of territory is not just driven by demographic need. Understanding the dynamics of land grabbing enables us to decode the nature of power and the character of society in the 21st century.

Taking life-giving land from others was a complicated business even for the perpetrators. The British were not alone in this venture.

---
1 Freeman (1869: 28-29), quote in Ward-Perkins (2005: 5-7).
2 Spencer (1851: 114-15).

> In the Americas, the Spanish appropriated both metallic wealth and an indigenous population to extract it. The Dutch appropriated routes, connections, to sustain commerce. The English appropriated territory, which required that they find ways either of sharing it with a pre-existing population or of de-populating it – mostly the latter.[3]

Given that land grabbing is a painful business, a variety of coping techniques had to be employed.

> Force, obviously, is one major instrumentality. But at least as important are the techniques that permit one to plan, explain and justify one's appropriation, to and for oneself. Colonisation, this suggests, has an epistemology of its own – a theory of knowing that enable the processes of 'discovery' and ordering (or more accurately re-ordering) inherent in appropriation to take place.[4]

Breaking down this process to its major elements is the first step towards understanding the impact of colonisation. We are aided by Carl Schmitt, who defined colonialism as "nothing other than the odium of appropriation". He elaborated his point in an essay in 1957:

> We have no right to close our eyes to the problem of appropriation, and to refuse to think any more about it, because what one today calls world history in the West and the East is the history of development in the objects, means, and forms of appropriation interpreted as progress. This development proceeds from the *land-appropriations* of nomadic and agrarian-feudal times to the *sea-appropriations* of the 16th to the 19th century, over the *industry-appropriations* of the industrial-technical age and its distinction between developed and under-

---

3 Tomlins (2001: 26).
4 Tomlins (2001: 27).

developed areas, and, finally, to the *air-appropriations* and *space-appropriations* of the present.[5]

Anthropologically speaking, people established their sovereign claim to land by naming it. "A land-appropriation is constituted only if the appropriator is able to give the land a name."[6] Naming the territory was a sacred act, one that united nature with its occupants in what became a social space.

Western ideology has attempted to bring controversies over this history of appropriation to a philosophical end, by pretending that the process is now outmoded.

> As a consequence, appropriation becomes outmoded, even criminal, and division [of land] is no longer a problem, given the abundance. There is only production, only the problem-less fortune of pure consumption. No longer are there wars and crises, because unchained production no longer is partial and unilateral, but has become total and global…in a world created by man for himself…man can *give* without *taking*".[7]

But Schmitt did not penetrate deeper than his recognition that power was linked in a sinister way with land appropriation, a power that tended towards secrecy within government. The limits to his account of land appropriation are revealed by the concept of freedom, which he defines in terms of the separation of economics from politics. He draws a distinction between private and public law. We shall see, however, that this distinction is actually at the heart of the continuation of land appropriation. *We need to name this form of appropriation if the violence that continues to be associated with land grabbing is to be brought to an end.*

Colonialism's initial act was, indeed, one of forcefully negating other people's rights, including their identity. This happened in the

---

5 Schmitt (2006: 347). Emphasis in original.
6 Schmitt (2006: 348).
7 Schmitt (2006: 347).

New Jersey region of North America. The territory was occupied by aboriginals who claimed to be the first settlers. The Algonkin speaking tribes named themselves the *Lenape*. This translates into Original People. This was not a meaning that sat comfortably with the colonial settlers: it created psychological discomfort – a cognitive dissonance which required adjustment. The white settlers chose to rename them as Delaware, and transfer ownership of the territory by renaming it.

We are told that the Lenape were peaceful people; warfare was not characteristic "before the coming of Europeans, although there certainly were cases of raids on and by bands and rivalry over favoured hunting and fishing grounds and the like".[8]

The notion of permanent individual land ownership prevented a meeting of minds between the Indians and Europeans.

> Whites attempted, with success, to alienate Indian lands permanently, quickly, and with as little expense as possible. Generous quantities of rum were made available, often technically illegally, to hasten the process and through liquor as well as the lack of resistance to European diseases, the Lenape began to decline in numbers. Land alienation and the increasing tide of whites also served to encourage most surviving Indians to leave for the west.[9]

The project of the incomers was grounded in corruption: an inhuman disregard for the dignity of the original occupants, a devious disregard for their rights, a manipulative use of ideology to justify a fraudulent occupation of land. This was the deployment of violence at all its levels, psychological as well as physical, to acquire that which was required by others to sustain their game-dependent cultures.

It need not have been like this. It was possible to construct an arrangement based on mutual interest. For example, the first settlers were not able to take short cuts to the opportunities provided by nature. They were obliged to work. How hard they laboured depended

---

8   Wacker (1975: 87).
9   Wacker (1975: 119).

on the fruitfulness of nature. Hunting and gathering was labour-intensive, requiring an acute understanding of the ecological niche and a willingness to integrate with nature to ensure that her riches returned with seasonal regularity. The newcomers brought with them technologies that could have been shared with the first settlers in return for specialist knowledge about the local resources. Everyone would have benefited. Instead of aggregating the opportunities, however, the doctrine of exclusive possession drove the newcomers to demean the incumbents (see Box 4:1).

But colonialism was animated by people who believed they were superior to those whom they intended to displace. One outcome was the exploitation of the labour of others, to facilitate the territorial expansion. The majority of whites who arrived in North America were unwilling to work with, and integrate themselves into, a community that respected the first settlers. They had herded tribes on to reservations. Having taken their land, there was no reason to spare their lives.

Box 4:1   The Indian "Menace"

LANGUAGE betrays the prejudices of land grabbers. In Illinois in the 1840s, for example, Douglas McManis reports the new settlers' need for "the removal of the Indian Menace".[1]

Judged in ecological terms, who were the menace? Indians did not waste nature's resources. The white settlers, however, included speculators who intervened and "acquired vast holdings, which because of the prices demanded for land tended to keep legitimate settlers out of areas where such holdings were numerous".[2]

Speculation damaged everyone's interests. Indians were displaced, but Europeans were excluded on the whim of speculators who, seeking the highest price, kept land idle. This quarantining of land displaced Indians further westwards.

Net effect: scarce capital was wasted and land was held out of use, while the right of people to earn a living was abused. This behaviour was masked by those who promoted the problem in terms of the Indian "menace".

1 McManis (1964: 17).   2 McManis (1964: 63).

Such episodes, with variations in the detail, were played out on all continents by those who implemented Europe's colonial project. But is it fair to claim, as I do, that a forceful rearrangement of the social space necessarily reshapes the attitudes and culture which we have inherited? Contemporary cases illustrate this thesis. The example of Canada is poignant. (see Box 4:2).

But this history cannot be dismissed as an episode of the past. The deeds of appropriation have not come to an end. The form has mutated, but the essence of grabbing other people's territories remains alive.

Box 4:2

THE Canadian technique for erasing the rights of the first settlers became known as "kill the Indian in the child".

In the 19th century, Canadian governments paid churches to run residential schools for aboriginal children, who were removed from indigenous communities for all but a few months each year. Aboriginal languages were banned, and many pupils were psychologically, physically and sexually abused. Duncan Campbell-Scott (1862-1947), who ran the residential school programme in the 1920s as Head of the Department of Indian Affairs, used his command of language (he was a poet) to dramatise their project. Scott expressed the philosophy of these schools in these terms:

> I want to get rid of the Indian problem. I do not think as a matter of fact, that the country ought to continuously protect a class of people who are able to stand alone… Our objective is to continue until there is not a single Indian in Canada that has not been absorbed into the body politic and there is no Indian question, and no Indian Department.'

About 150,000 children attended the schools in a programme of indoctrination that was calculated to annihilate their culture. The last school was closed in the mid-1990s.[2]

1 Leslie (1978: 114).
2 Stephen Harper, Canada's Prime Minister, apologised to the country's aboriginals in Parliament on June 11, 2008 (Mason [2008]).

Early in the 20th century, critics of capitalism like J.A. Hobson (1858-1940) and V.I. Lenin (1870-1924) noted that Europe and North America had originated a new phase of imperialism just as the expansion of their territories was coming to an end.[10] They defined imperialism as finance capitalism. Revenue was extracted out of the colonial (and now the neo-colonial) countries through the financial sector, by means that perpetrate the exploitation of land and the indigenous peoples.

Colonialism evolved into its purest expression when it found ways to extract rent without having to incur the costs of owning, or administering, land itself. Rent is the value which we all participate in creating, through our activities in community. It is the *public* value, which we jointly create through the fusion of our *private* activities with our collective investment in public services. However, to administer such services, we require the engagement of public agencies. Thus, Schmitt was not correct when he defined freedom in terms of "the separation of economics and politics, of private and public law, [which] still today is considered by noted teachers of law to be an essential guarantee of freedom".[11] Quite the contrary, *freedom requires the integration of the principles of liberty with the economic efficiencies of the market to yield the optimum social surplus.* For this surplus to be reinvested for the common good (which is a pre-condition for achieving the desired wealth and welfare), we require the correct integration of public and private law.

In Part IV, we investigate the claim that the association of land and tax policies affords the final solution to the generalised violence that will otherwise remain ingrained in modern society. But first, we need to further explore the consequences of colonialism through its expression of violence in the neo-colonial era.

---

10 Hobson's classic was *Imperialism: A Study* (1902). Lenin followed this with *Imperialism, the Highest Stage of Capitalism* (1916).
11 Schmitt (2006: 340).

Kenya: paradigm of neo-colonialism[12]

THE territory in East Africa now known as Kenya has been subject to at least three waves of people claiming the use of land. That history illustrates how land tenure, when it is not correctly defined as the synthesis of a person's private and public rights, perpetuates a continuous process of violence. We pick up the story with the arrival from the south of white settlers who coveted the lush terrain. Vast expanses of land could be converted from pastoral to agricultural use. But who would undertake the labour on the land, and on what terms?

The attitudes and institutions of the British colonial administration were identified with brutal honesty by Sir Percy Girouard, Governor of the Protectorate, in a statement that was reported in the *East African Standard* on February 8, 1913. He declared:

> We consider that the only natural and automatic method of securing a constant labour supply is to ensure that there shall be competition among labourers for hire and not among employers for labourers; such competition can be brought about only by a rise in the cost of living for the native, and this rise can be produced only by an increase in the tax.[13]

Hijacking the labour of others was the objective, but this could not be achieved without the connivance of the state. First, people had to be displaced. Some were herded on to reserves, so that their land could be appropriated. But here the Africans could still work land for their subsistence, rather than submitting to service on white farms as indentured labourers. The policy challenge was to rig the rules to deny people the freedom to continue to earn an independent living.

A two-pronged attack was adopted. First, restrictions were placed on the ability of Africans to grow cash crops, so that their households could not become viable economic units. But it went further than that: they even had to be prevented from earning a subsistence lifestyle. Some labourers had to be coerced off the land and on to the estates

---

12 Neo-colonialism is defined in Harrison (2008).
13 Manners (1962: 497).

to work for white farmers. The solution was an elegant partnership between commerce and the colonial state. This is how that relationship was developed.

Commerce made available goods that could only be acquired for cash. By this means, the consumption requirements of the indigenous population were altered. But the new needs could only be satisfied if they had cash in their pockets. What would drive peasants off their subsistence holdings and into the cash economy? The state intervened with its powers of taxation. It imposed a tax on huts. This was later joined by the Poll Tax – the price on a person's head. In order to meet these fiscal obligations, Africans were obliged to seek wage labour on white farms.

> Thus, if the imposition of taxes together with a shrunken land base seemed unlikely to generate a large labor force at low wage rates, it might be hoped that an efficient internal marketing system would help to deal with the problem.[14]

The technique was to restrict economic freedom and twist the culture of the Africans by hooking them into the Western economy as consumers. By this means, they became a dependent labour force. They were forced to bid down their wages. Employers, on the other hand, would be protected from having to bid up remuneration to *attract* people off the land. Thus was created the unequal relationship dictated by the abusive form of land tenure that was reinforced by state-directed tax policy to accommodate the land grabbers.

The circumstances of the dispossessed did not improve after Kenya became a sovereign nation, however. The failure of successive governments to address the land question culminated in inter-tribal conflicts in shanty towns in 2008, and the deaths of more than 1,000 people. This legacy over the unfinished business of land reform was not unique to Kenya, as we shall see in the case of Guatemala.

---

14 Manners (1962: 498).

Guatemala: structured anarchy

THE failures of diplomacy to resolve disputes in regions torn by contests over land are dramatised by Guatemala.

Over 42,000 people died in that country's civil conflict, which lasted from 1960 to 1996. According to a report on the treatment of Mayan Indians, extermination was regarded as a legitimate practice against innocent people. In attempting to control the territory and prevent change to property rights, indigenous communities had to be suppressed. The army viewed Mayans as natural allies of the guerrillas. They expressed their animosity in racist terms, rather than conceding that theirs was a contest for control of land, which

> led to the extermination *en masse*, of defenceless Mayan communities purportedly linked to the guerrillas – including children, women and the elderly – through methods whose cruelty has outraged the moral conscience of the civilised world…In the majority of massacres there is evidence of multiple acts of savagery, which preceded, accompanied or occurred after the deaths of the victims. Acts such as the killing of defenceless children, often by beating them against walls or throwing them alive into pits where the corpses of adults were later thrown…[15]

The combatants sought a peace accord in 1996. This was supposed to address social and economic issues. The taboo subject, however, was land reform. Although the issue was raised, the diplomacy was confined to privatisation of land. This made it difficult to resettle the refugees who had fled to neighbouring countries.

The only way to establish citizenship and overcome economic marginalisation was to acquire land. But the peace agreement of 1992 failed to define land rights in a way that would obviate further social tensions. One outcome was yet further civil aggression along the Guatemalan border as refugees attempted to appropriate land. In one location where they purchased land, the inhabitants of neighbouring

---

15 Guatemalan Commission for Historical Clarification (2007), cited in Taylor (2009: 5-6).

villages became hostile: they resented the fact that the refugees were able to acquire land with soft loans from foreign governments when they had previously failed to obtain the credit needed to purchase the hectares which they occupied. There were also problems due to the difficulty of establishing documentary evidence of legal title. Consequently, faced with threats from 200 men from one village, the refugees fled.

In the event, in this one case, the land was divided. But its price was set too high for the existing villagers. The refugees, however, because of their access to loans on easy terms, were able to purchase their half of the land. The remainder was left vacant.[16]

Thus, tenurial rights confined the outcome to one that relied on the application of violence, with the wasteful misuse of land as a by-product. A Danish researcher who observed the dispute at close quarters reports: "The villagers lost the conflict. But now everybody knows that there will be trouble if they try to buy the land. So violence is used to establish possession of the land. In the transition from [civil] conflict to peace, it is interesting to see how violence is used and talked about. It is paradoxical; because the institutions tried to outlaw violence and monopolise it – only the state can use it".[17] Far from being paradoxical, under the model based on exclusive ownership the use of violence is an integral tool for establishing dominance over land, and therefore the people on the territory.

The issues were complicated by the claims of a former owner who had left the area and then returned to assert the rights which he had previously neglected. Overlaying this legal issue were the demographic needs of both the present generation of landless citizens, and those of future generations.

This Guatemalan case highlights the inefficiencies of the private property model of rights in countries struggling to develop.

- *Ecologically*, it is inefficient in the use of land. Significant parts of the domain are left vacant because the price is unaffordable to some prospective users.

---

16 Stepputat (2007).
17 Stepputat (2007).

- *Socially*, deficiencies in property rights must necessarily be reflected in the flawed character of the culture and communities that do succeed in establishing themselves.
- *Institutionally*, chaos reigns in the way that ownership is determined, and in the way that land is measured and proprietary rights are recorded.
- *Economically*, many people are marginalised, encouraging them to turn to drug smuggling and people trafficking across the border to Mexico, in transit to the USA.

The result is anarchy. The supplanting society paradigm (see Chapter 5), it appears, is bereft of strategies for resolving problems in the 21st century. For the politics of that society is predicated on appropriation and privatisation, with the emphasis on exclusivity of ownership (exclusion) rather than inclusivity. This creates stress at the urban political centre, where the instruments of coercion are exercised, and instability at the economic margin. This is a formula for permanent chaos.

Globally, the outcome of colonisation is a 200-year history of increasing inequality. The evidence is revealed by the growing gap between the incomes of the rich and poor, and the statistical index known as the Gini coefficient in which perfect equality is put at zero (Table 4:1). The higher the number (moving towards 1, or unity), the higher the inequality.

Table 4:1 Global Inequality (1820-1992)

	1820	1850	1870	1890	1910	1929	1950	1960	1970	1980	1992
Ratio of income of top 5% to bottom 20% of individuals	7	7	9	10	12	12	15	14	16	18	16
Gini coefficient	0.5	0.532	0.56	0.588	0.61	0.616	0.64	0.635	0.65	0.657	0.657

Sources: Calculated from Bourguignon and Morrison (2002: 731-732, Table 1) and cited in Jolly (2005: 15).

The supplanting process, as a technique for eviscerating identity and culture, continues to this day in all parts of the world. We hear of the contests over land only when violence erupts and people die, as happened when Muslims and Hindus clashed in Indian-administered Kashmir in June 2008. The cause of the dispute was a government plan to dispose of 40 acres of forest land which contained a sacred site. The Muslims felt that their culture (and the demographic composition of the territory) was threatened by the political initiative; people died, and one observer explained: "Land is a very sensitive issue in Kashmir. The people feel they've already lost a lot, and if now their land also goes, then everything is gone".[18] Any solution to the history of deprivation must accept the fluid movement of people on Earth within an institutional framework that enables populations to *co-exist* with, rather than *supplant*, others.

---

18 Rahman (2008).

CHAPTER 5

THE PATHOLOGY OF RE-ORDERED SPACE

THE concept of "supplanting" societies is a useful diagnostic tool. It offers a sense of the dynamics of the nation-state built on the land-grab ethic. David Day uses the concept to summarise history in terms of two phases.

- First, expansion onto virgin territory. This began in Africa. It entailed the adjustment of human capabilities to the ecological niche. This included the physical adaptation to nature, to fulfil emerging needs; a process that continued as humans fanned out from the Rift Valley, in the area stretching from Kenya to Ethiopia, to the rest of the world.
- The second wave was based on the model of "supplanting" communities from their ecological niches. Settlers discovered that they were not the first to reach the "new" or "undiscovered" territories. Their arrival entailed the displacement (or absorption) of the first settlers. Integral to the redefinition of the right of occupation was the violation of the rights of others.

In Day's view, "the history of most societies can be best understood when they are seen as part of a never-ending struggle, in a world of shifting boundaries, to make particular territories their own".[1] But

---
1 Day (2008: 7).

the "supplanting" process was not confined to the arrival of outsiders, who dislodged the first settlers. Supplanting also occurs in established societies where tenurial rights are rewritten to serve the interests of a minority. There may come a time when one group attempts to re-arrange the occupation of its territory. The newly created space is then occupied by the victors.

Nazi Germany fine-tuned the technologies for re-ordering the living space. Adolph Hitler was an ambitious land grabber. First, he launched his army to appropriate land to the east of Germany. Then, adopting the industrial process of gas chambers, he sought to expand the space available on the home territory for Aryan children.

The darkest side to European colonisation was the displacement of existing occupants. Officially, these land grabs were justified by claiming that people were being civilised. The practical consequence was the systematic killing of people. The scale of the slaughters remains controversial, but the order of magnitude – summarised in Table 5:1 – leaves no doubt that killing was not a by-product of the appropriation of land; it was integral to the business of re-ordering the definition and use of space.

Table 5:1   Tribal Depopulation: Some Estimates

	Pre-Contact Population	Population Low Point	Depopulation
US & Canada	9,800,000	490,000	9,310,000
Lowland South America	9,000,000	450,000	8,550,000
Polynesia	1,100,000	180,000	920,000
Micronesia	200,000	83,000	117,000
Fiji	300,000	85,000	215,000
New Caledonia	100,000	27,000	73,000
Australia	300,000	60,500	239,500
Congo	N/A	N/A	8,000,000?
		Estimated Total Depopulation	27,860,000

Source: Bodley (1982: 40). These estimates are subject to considerable uncertainty. For the French Congo, for example, the depopulation between 1900 and 1921 may have been as much as 12m souls.

Killing as a policy tool receives insufficient attention in the history books, but some historians are well aware that colonies could only be created at a high human price. Cambridge scholar Robin Bidwell was emphatic in his assessment. He studied the impact on the tribes of Morocco when the French decided to impose their civilisation on the Berbers and Arabs who live in the north-west corner of the African continent. Drawing on archives in Paris, he quotes one official as acknowledging that conquest without colonisation left no more lasting mark on the land than the wake of a ship on the sea.

> History suggests that European colonisation can only really be permanent and successful when, as in the United States, the original population is practically exterminated. In America this was even a matter for pride, for many followed Theodore Roosevelt in believing that 'this great Continent could not have been kept as nothing but a game reserve for squalid savages'.[2]

The popular histories that have been converted into colourful images on television focus on the genocide perpetrated by Nazi Germany. Almost no treatment is accorded the genocides in the rest of the world by Europe's colonial powers. An example was the mass extermination of tribal peoples (mainly the Herero) by the German army in South-West Africa (Namibia) in the three years following 1904.[3]

Evidence for the barbarity associated with the civilising process abounds. The problem with the compilation of anecdotal evidence, however, is that the horror of that evidence distracts us from the use of violence as a process that was institutionalised into the modern system of land tenure. Kathleen Taylor, for example, recalls the horror orchestrated by a Peruvian corporation (backed by British investors) who used the Huitoto Indians as forced labour on their rubber plantations in the Amazon at the beginning of the 20th century. An American adventurer, Walter Hardenburg, reported observing how

---

2 Bidwell (1973: 199).
3 Balfour (1997: Ch. 1).

> Peaceful Indians were put to work at rubber-gathering without payment, without food, in nakedness; that their women were stolen, ravished, and murdered; that the Indians were flogged until their bones were laid bare when they failed to bring in a sufficient quota of rubber or attempted to escape, were left to die with their wounds festering with maggots, and their bodies were used as food for the agents' dogs…target-shooting for diversion was practised upon them, and they were soused in petroleum and burned alive, both men and women.[4]

Such evidence, however, was not used to reform the doctrines on which modern property rights relied. Consequently, the same strategies were used in the post-colonial era. This included murderous tactics employed in the civil war of Democratic Kampuchea during the early 1970s, in which up to 2m people were killed in four years – an average of 1,000 a day. In Rwanda in 1994, genocide claimed 800,000 people in 100 days. We can derive no comfort from being reminded that such behaviour was not a modern innovation, that Julius Caesar "wiped out entire tribes, killing many and selling the rest into slavery"[5] (see Box 5:1).

The appropriation of territory created complications that spawned unique solutions. To execute the land grab, people had to be expelled from the enclosed space. But unless the new settlers were to labour on the land themselves, they had to enlist the labour of others. Employing the displaced population may create a problem, for the victims posed a continuing threat to the land grabbers. The traditional association with the land remained a source of emotional and spiritual strength, an attachment which nourished the hope that, one day, birthrights would be reclaimed. So it could be dangerous to retain displaced people on the land as tenants or labourers.

So labour was imported. That labour needed to be demoralised, bereft of the aspiration to become independent users of land. The

---

4 Quoted in Taylor (2009: 260).
5 Taylor (2009: 259).

THE PATHOLOGY OF RE-ORDERED SPACE 61

> **Box 5:1 Slavery**
>
> SLAVERY was a feature of Athenian society and Roman imperialism. European traffic in negroes originated with the Portuguese in 1442, but was developed only after the discovery of America. The trade was conducted by the English, French and Dutch. Under the Treaty of Utrecht (1713), Spain signed an exclusive contract (the Asiento) to supply English colonies with slaves.
>
> The trade encouraged tribal chiefs on the Slave Coast (the Cameroons, Angola and their hinterlands) to kidnap people to supply the markets at the ports. One result was the implosion of communities and the economic ruin of large areas of West Africa.
>
> Enslavement was not confined to Africans. English criminals and political prisoners were sent as slaves to the plantations in the New World in the 17th century. The kidnapping of English children for sale continued up to 1744.
>
> Christians were not alone in facilitating the institution of slavery. Muslims engaged in the trade. A poignant case is described by Des Ekin, in which raiders from Algiers and troops of the Turkish Ottoman Empire captured nearly all of the inhabitants of Baltimore, a harbour village in West Cork, Ireland, and sold them in North Africa.[1]
>
> [1] Ekin (2006).

importation of labour from a far away place – creating a psychologically disorientated, culturally impoverished and dependent group of hostage workers - was a logical strategy. Men and women who were kidnapped from their homelands were dumped in alien environments across the oceans with no cultural bearings to orientate their minds. They were auctioned for their muscle power alone. The re-conditioning of that labour began on the long passage from West Africa to the New World. An estimated 1m slaves are thought to have died on the ships crossing the Atlantic, some of them thrown overboard after falling sick. Then, when the economics of plantations changed, the enforced labour could be abandoned in favour of new devices of exploitation, such as the importation of indentured labour from Asia.

The legacy was not just the damage to the victimised populations. The colonisers also had to abuse themselves, if they were to efficiently carry out the project of grabbing the land of others. The psychological costs cannot be measured; but they can be traced in the language that was evolved to register the disrespect for other humans.

The Language of Violence

THE exploitation of land as a process is mirrored in the psychology of the individuals who wrought the changes. This was a personal necessity to enable the perpetrators to cope with the inhumanity of their actions: the mind-set had to be reshaped to accommodate the structure of property rights. This was necessary, because the new land ethic was not a one-off historical event: it would have to be continuously refreshed, not least by administering the fiscal policies on which the property rights relied for the maldistribution of income.

Everyone suffered. The loss of humanity was a price paid by the colonists who built the British empire. In degrading others, they demeaned their own moral character. This process is now called "otherization". But the cruelty is insufficiently explained by scholars like Kathleen Taylor, who analyse it in terms of neuroscience.[6] They describe the physical violence associated with otherization as a consequence of linguistic and attitudinal acts, and therefore distinct from the displacement of people from their land. Our case study is 18th century Jamaica, the island of sugar plantations described by Edward Long in a three-volume study published in 1774.[7]

Long was the son of a plantation owner who married into a family which owned over 44,000 acres in 1750. He was trained as a barrister in London, but took up his inheritance on the death of his father in 1757. He was engaged in the boom in production which saw the number of sugar plantations increase from 419 to 775 in the middle of the 18th century, supported by a slave population that doubled from 100,000 to 197,000 souls.

In seeking to understand the attitudes and actions of people like Long, we may read his treatise as addressing two problems. First, a psychological tension existed among people who regarded themselves

---

6 Taylor (2009).
7 Long, (2002).

as civilised, as the products of The Enlightenment. Given the idealism of that era, how could slavery be justified? This was a conundrum for plantation owners in North America who relied on slaves, but who used the slave analogy to dramatise what they perceived as their political subordination to a motherland that was taking liberties with their rights. The second problem was that, in 1772, a high court judgement outlawed slavery in Britain. This encouraged talk about the general abolition of slavery.

A cognitive adjustment to these two awkward issues was needed, and Long's study of Jamaica provided the rationalisation for peace of mind the slave owners needed. The first line of attack was to deny that the planters treated their negroes with barbarity.

Slave owners, Long insisted, were not "tyrants, inhuman oppressors, bloody inquisitors".[8] The planters, after all, did not enslave the Africans in the first place. Rather, they "succeeded to the inheritance of their services in the same manner as an English squire succeeds to the estate of his ancestors; and that, as to his Africans, he buys their services from those who have all along pretended a very good right to sell".[9] This was a dangerous line of argument for a lawyer to advance in the court of public opinion. For if it could not sustain the ownership of slaves, by association it could not legitimise the ownership of the land that was inherited from one's ancestors. But this was not a possibility that concerned Long; the right to enclose and privatise the commons of England was no longer effectively challenged by those who were dispossessed.

The legal argument, however, was not sufficient to overcome the cognitive dissonance associated with transgressing the rights of other human beings. Thus, Edward Long made plain the adjustments that had to be made to the relationship between white owner and black slave.

> The planters do not want to be told, that their Negroes are
> human creatures. If they believe them to be human kind,

---

8 Long, (2002: 267).
9 Long, (2002: 267).

they cannot regard them...as no better than dogs or horses. But how many poor wretches, even in England, are treated with far less care and humanity than these brute animals![10]

Enslaved persons were dehumanised (see Box 5:2). They were not like the white owners. As evidence, Long cited the problems that arose when the offspring of the plantation owners associated with these "brute animals". White children were exposed to domestic servants "whose drawling, dissonant gibberish they insensibly adopt, and with it no small tincture of their awkward carriage and vulgar manners; all which they do not easily get rid of, even after an English education, unless sent away extremely young".[11]

That was one reason why, even when emancipated, former slaves needed to be segregated from whites. They could not be treated as equals under the law "for they were not supposed to have acquired any sense of morality by the mere act of manumission".[12] By such reasoning, it was possible to justify their disqualification from giving evidence against whites in a court of law. And they were not permitted to vote at parochial or general elections. It was different if they inherited large estates from their former masters. Ownership of land qualified them to act as if they were human.[13] Humanity was directly pegged to the association with land.

Only whites, however, could be safely entrusted with substantial holdings of land. From five to ten acres of land were sufficient for one freed Negro. But, from the public interest point of view, "it is better that the Negro should continue an honest and industrious slave, than to be turned into an idle and profligate free man".[14] And that was why a law needed to be passed to prevent Negroes from acquiring substantial estates.

Long chronicled the risks of cross-breeding. In the Spanish colonies, this had led to the birth of "a vicious, brutal, and degenerate breed of

---

10 Long (2002: 270).
11 Long (2002: 278).
12 Long (2002: 320).
13 Long (2002: 321-322).
14 Long (2002: 323).

Box 5:2   Images of Humanity

FROM the earliest European contacts, the people of Africa were branded as sub-human. The more open-minded travellers revealed a rich culture in the "dark continent". One of these was the first champion of the negroes of South Africa, Johannes Gulielmus de Grevenbroek. He attacked the "half-truths" spread in Europe about Africans, whom he found

> living in harmony with nature's law, hospitable to every race of men, open, dependable, lovers of truth and justice, not utterly unacquainted with the worship of some God, endowed...with a rare nimbleness of mother wit, and having minds receptive of instruction...it is through the faults of our countrymen...that the natives have been changed for the worse...From us they have learned...misdeeds unknown to them before, and, among other crimes of deepest die, the accursed lust for gold.[1]

By the 18th century, the falsehoods had shifted markedly. The "noble savage" became a theme in the accounts of travellers. This notion, however, may have had less to do with a deeper understanding of life in Africa and America, and more to do with the degeneration of culture in Europe. Katherine George suggests that the noble savage concept arose from "a definite dissatisfaction with the inadequacies and injustices of Western civilization",[2] offering an oblique critique of the European way of life, which the amateur anthropologists were able to contrast with what they observed on other continents. In particular, the qualities that the travellers admired in the African character included

> his hospitality, his love of his fellows and his generous sharing with them, his lack of envy and avarice. The qualities of primitive African society which tend to be similarly exalted are its freedom, its equalitarianism, its responsiveness to the needs and desires of all its members. One also often hears of the absence among primitive Africans of some foolish prohibition or unnatural restriction which in civilized society obstructs the course of life.[3]

1 Grevenbroek (1958: 69).   2 George (1958: 71).   3 George (1958: 71).

---

mongrels" – the offspring of Spaniards, blacks, Indians, and their mixed progeny.[15] His clinching argument for legitimising the ownership of

---

15   Long, (2002: 327).

others, to shackled them to the land as beasts of burden, was that "the white and the Negro are two distinct species".[16] This accounted for the differences in intellect. Dutifully trawling all the information available from the early land grabbers who had turned themselves into amateur anthropologists and historians, Long concluded that the Negroes preferred "their savage way of life"[17] rather than adopt a settled existence on 20 acres of land.

To animate the white mind into a state of resignation with, and acceptance of, this form of property ownership, Long described how negroes displayed the kind of agility that invited comparisons with animals "They skip about like so many monkies".[18] He compared the regions of Africa from which the slaves had been kidnapped, and it appeared that the Angolans were "the most stupid of the Negro race, are the most offensive; and those of Senegal (who are distinguished from the other herds by greater acuteness of understanding and mildness of disposition) have the least…noxious odour".[19]

> In general, they are void of genius, and seem almost incapable of making any progress on civility or science. They have no plan or system of morality among them. Their barbarity to their children debases their nature even below that of brutes. They have no moral sensations; no taste but for women; gormondizing, and drinking to excess; no wish but to be idle.[20]

Referring to Africa, Long concluded that

> Whatever great personages this country might anciently have produced, and concerning whom we have no information, they are now every where degenerated into a brutish, ignorant, idle, crafty, treacherous, bloody, thievish, mistrustful, and superstitious people, even in those states

---
16 Long, (2002: 336).
17 Long, (2002: 339).
18 Long, (2002: 349).
19 Long, (2002: 353).
20 Long, (2002: 353).

where we might expect to find them more polished, humane, docile, and industrious.[21]

This was the appraisal of a civilised Englishman of not much more than two centuries ago. Awkwardly, back in England, the son of an African was being feted in the salons of the upper classes (see box 5:3). Such evidence, however, would not distract the plantation owners. Long explained that even if we had to acknowledge that some tribes had displayed skills of mechanical arts or of manufacturing, these skills were "not better than an *oran-utang* might, with a little pains, be brought to do".[22] By degrading the Europeans' perception of Africans, plantation owners like Edward Long could assert that

> When we reflect on the nature of these men, and their dissimilarity to the rest of mankind, must we not conclude, that they are a different species of the same *genus*?[23]

Box 5:3   Beethoven's Friend

GEORGE BRIDGETOWER was born in 1779, the son of an Abyssinian ex-West Indian slave. He was a child prodigy on the violin. His performances as a ten-year old in Paris before the French revolution were acclaimed. After he sought refuge in London, he was adopted by the Prince of Wales. He played in the Prince's band at the Royal Pavilion, Brighton, for 14 years.

His mastery of music was celebrated when Ludwig von Beethoven wrote a new piece – the Kreutzer Sonata – for the Afro-European violinist. Mulatto he may have been, reported the Bath Chronicle (December 3, 1789), but the violinist's exquisite performance was "perhaps superior, to the best professor of the present day or any former day".

Bridgewater died in poverty in South London in 1860, having proved that his ancestral blood was every bit as capable of achieving the highest aesthetic accomplishments on display in "polite society".

Bridgewater featured in an exhibition on London's Tower Bridge in July 2007, which was held to mark the abolition of the Slave Trade Act (1807).

---

21 Long, (2002: 354).
22 Long (2002: 355).
23 Long (2002: 356).

In concluding that whites were a superior species, Long violated the integrity of the European mind itself. To legitimise a doctrine of property rights that was necessitated by the monopoly control of land, he violated the humanity of the oppressors.

Edward Long was not an evil person. He was socialised by an ideology that had to defend itself by any means. This included the self-flagellation of the mind and of the morals of those who abused the humanity of others. This mentality was carried over to the institutions and politics of the 20th century.

CHAPTER 6

GENOCIDE & THE CONCENTRATION CAMP

WHEN Europe's Great Powers reached the outer limits of global expansion, their state constitution left them with no choice but to turn their territorial ambitions inwards on each other. This was the story of the 20th century. The spatial conflicts were played out in the wars of two ideologies – capitalism and communism – with dead people as the necessary by-product of the struggle to re-order the European space. Table 6:1 offers estimates of the number of victims. The actual numbers cannot be computed with accuracy. Matthew White offers a comprehensive survey of the published evidence in his on-line *Historical Atlas of the 20th Century*.[1] Killing was on an industrial scale, and genocide featured as a necessary element of the process. Civilians were part of the "collateral damage" of set-piece military conflicts. As good an estimate of the number of victims as we can get appears to be around the 180m mark (Table 6:1).

Table 6:1   Deaths by War and Oppression: the 20th century record (millions)

Mode of Killing	Total
Genocide & Tyranny	83
Military Wars	42
Civilian Deaths in Wars	19
Man-made Famines	44
Total	188

Source: White (2001).

1   White (2001).

Can we really account for these tragedies in terms of a single causal mechanism? Historians, because they tend to confine their descriptions to observable events, would dismiss my hypothesis as superficial. So it would pay to refer back to the foundation texts. In particular, given that communism was inspired by hostility to capitalism, what did Karl Marx say about the internal dynamics of the capitalist system?

Marx stressed the role of *capital* – the man-made tools for adding value to the wealth of the nation. His 3-volume work was called *Das Kapital*. If he had called it, say, *The Monopoly of Land*, the 20th century might have taken an entirely different course. But he didn't do so, of course, so what do we learn from his theoretical framework?

Capital, it appears, far from being the instrument for exploiting the working class, was itself the victim of a prior set of values. Capitalists, in their role as producers of goods (recognising that many capitalists were also significant land owners) were exploited by land owners who offered land on predatory terms. Insofar as employers *were* able to take advantage of their employees, this was predicated on the prior displacement of people from the land they needed to create independent ways of earning a living.

In *Critique of the Gotha Programme*, Marx wrote the words which are popularly accepted as representing the structure of power in capitalism: "In present-day society the instruments of labour are the monopoly of the landowners *and* the capitalists".

Marxist scholarship and ideological pamphlets of the past century have been based on the premise that wicked employers were the architects of the terrible deeds of exploitation inflicted on the working class. But Marx qualified his statement. The words he added in brackets stood the whole Marxist structure on its head. He wrote:

> ...the monopoly of property in land is even the basis of the monopoly of capital...[2]

The overriding power in the capitalist economy was in the hands of land monopolists. Factory owners of the early Industrial Revolution

---
2 Marx (1973b: 19). Emphasis in original

were as exposed to that primary form of privileged power as the landless labourers who crammed into the towns searching for work. Marx wrote: "In England, the capitalist is usually not even the owner of the land on which his factory stands".[3] So, as I have previously written, "the power wielded by capital was derivative, of a secondary nature, and *not* intrinsic to itself: if labour was vulnerable to capital, then, it was because workers did not have access to land of their own".[4]

Marx did appreciate the significance of what he was saying in that parenthetical aside in his *Critique*. What, for example, would happen if land were re-socialised? This is what he stated in answer to that question:

> The nationalisation of land will work a complete change in the relations between labour and capital, and finally, do away with the capitalist form of production, whether industrial or rural.[5]

With this observation, Marx swept aside the crudities of the Marxist doctrine that advocated the wholesale nationalisation of the means of production. All that was needed was a mechanism for drawing the social benefits of land back into the public domain where they originated. If that was done, the predators would not be able to exploit others, no matter how much capital they might have accumulated. Marx indicated as much when he turned his attention to the process of colonisation, where the white settlers had access to plenty of land. For capital to have the power of exploitation, it was first necessary to place land beyond the reach of labour. This is how Marx put it:

> ...the capitalist finds that his capital *ceases to be capital* without wage labour, and that one of the pre-suppositions of the latter is not only landed property in general, but modern landed property; landed property which, as capitalized rent,

---

3 This was generally the case throughout the Old World. In the New World, as described below, capitalists competed with land speculators for control over prime locations and natural resources.
4 Harrison (1979: 211).
5 Marx (1973a: 290).

is expensive, and which, as such, excludes the direct use of the soil by individuals. Hence Wakefield's theory of colonies, followed in practise by the English government in Australia. Landed property is here artificially made more expensive in order to transform the workers into wage-workers, to make capital *act as capital*.[6]

If Lenin *et al* had read Marx's works more carefully, their challenge to capitalism might have been founded on a completely different basis. Whether that would have resulted in fewer deaths in the 20th century, we cannot know. Would the Maoist murders in China's countryside have been necessary, if the Chinese had liberated peasants by allowing them to work their land and keep the fruits of their labours, while contributing the rents to the public purse?[7] In any event, the predators of the 20th century were determined to cling to power at all costs. And genocide was one of the tools for doing so. A closer look at the dynamics of land appropriation reveals that what we today label as an *industrialised* process is associated with the pre-existing techniques of the land grabbers.

Concentration Camps

EARLY anthropologists understood that land tenure was a key buttress of society, without which the cultural edifice would collapse. Their studies showed how Europeans manipulated people's lives by interfering with the ancient tenurial rules that had safeguarded them through countless environmental and social challenges. An example is provided by the Lieutenant-Governor of the northern Provinces of Nigeria. In *Native Races and Their Rulers*, C.L. Temple wrote:

> There is no question of more importance to the European Administrator of African tribes than that of Land Tenure.

---

6 Marx 1973b: 278). Emphasis added.
7 In the *Communist Manifesto* (1848), Marx placed the re-socialisation of rent at the top of the list of reforms needed by a post-capitalist society. Russia's revolutionaries nationalised the land, but failed to distinguish between the collection of community-created rents, and privately created income.

> No subject bulks so large in the eyes of the native. Through no other channel of administration can a Government so completely establish satisfactorily the economic status and social relations of a native population or, on the contrary, so surely and completely reduce the natives to a state of poverty, mutual discord, grumbling and resentment against their rulers than by the adoption of right or wrong measures in respect to the tenure of land by natives.[8]

Colonial administrators understood the centrality of land tenure, but they were the instruments of a colonial project whose logic entailed the wrecking of the rules that filtered people's relationship with the land and ensured an orderly use of nature's resources.

The extension of an incoming group's power over the territory necessarily required the spatial retreat of the existing population. But the incumbents were not always willing to be displaced, so devices had to be employed that became hallmarks of the colonial land grab. The concentration camp was one such instrument. It was employed by Italy's Colonel Rodolfo Graziani during the occupation of North Africa in the 1920s.[9] And Britain used it to good effect in South Africa at the turn into the 20th century. David Hogg summarises the way the British herded people into concentration camps.

> There were 110,000 prisoners in the camps in 1902 and deaths averaged 250 a week. 27,000 people died in British Concentration Camps, many of them women and children. The Dutch were understandably very bitter and deeply resented the British invasion and annexation of their lands. Not only were the Boars imprisoned but also the indigenous population, and in fact there were 65 Black Concentration Camps, which is many more than the 47 Boer Camps. The statistics above do not include the African Camps.[10]

---

8 Temple (1918: 135).
9 Wright (1969: 177).
10 Hogg (2007: 126-127).

Using women and children as instruments of war, to displace those who claimed to possess the land, was profitable for the landlord class that controlled the British nation-state. They were the primary beneficiaries of the rents extracted from the territories of others. A sense of the magnitude of those rents is given by the value of diamonds extracted out of the De Beer's and Kimberly mines in the run-up to the use of concentration camps in South Africa. Table 6:1 provides the measure of the rents – in pounds, shillings and pence – of the diamond business.

Britain was not alone in using concentration camps as a tool for re-ordering the control of space. A few years earlier, Spain used economic warfare in Cuba, where Spanish troops employed the concentration camp model to herd civilians into confined spaces. This gave them a free hand "to burn crops, plantations, and villages, and kill whomsoever they came across".[11]

We overlook these episodes initiated by Europeans, preferring to recall more recent cases such as the tragedy of Rwanda. But, as we shall now see, that murderous episode cannot be understood without locating it in its colonial origins.

Table 6:1   Rents from the De Beers and Kimberly Diamond Mines

Year Ending	Amount Realised per load s. d.	Cost of Production per load s. d.	Rent per load s. d.	Dividends Paid: £	Equal to: %
1889	25 3¾	9 10½	15 5¼	188,329	5
1890	37 2¾	8 10½	28 4¼	789,682	20
1891	29 3¾	8 8	20 7¼	789,791	20
1892	23 5	7 4	16 1	1,382,135	35
1893	30 6	6 11	23 7	987,238	25
1894	21 10	6 6	15 4	987,238	25
1895	21 8	6 10	14 10	987,238	25
1896	24 4	7 0	17 4	1,579,152	40
1897	24 8	7 4	17 4	1,579,582	40
1898	21 2	6 7	14 7	1,579,582	40

Source: Creswicke (1900: 135).

---

11   Balfour (2002: 123).

Rwanda: the Culture of Discrimination

RWANDA serves as a notorious case for the anarchy which appears to validate racial prejudices. Today, people know it as a place where genocide was perpetrated in the 1990s. Hollywood brought the mass murders to the big screen in *Hotel Rwanda*. Tribal conflicts are used to subliminally justify the sense of racial superiority.

Repeated acts of mass slaughter are not consistent with "normal" behaviour. If there is such a thing as normality in relation to violent behaviour, we need to refer to the routine behaviour of the many territorial species in the animal kingdom. There, we observe that spatial boundaries are protected by acts of aggression which take the form of displays of physical postures and threatening noises. Wilful killing is absent, mass slaughter non-existent.

Humans had this instinct for preservation built into their genes. The symbolic gestures that were used to defend home territories were reinforced with rules and institutions, to ensure internal stability of clans and tribes, and co-existence with neighbouring tribes. Everyone knew his place, and mass killing was an aberration in the anthropological record. The general rule is a revealing one: the first drawing of blood was sufficient to terminate hostilities.

Evidence contrary to this general account can be found. But such evidence is the exception that supports the rule that pre-civilised humans did not engage in the barbaric behaviour that we associate with modern European history. So how, then, can we account for the horrendous crimes in Rwanda? Not, it seems, in the alleged evil of the individuals who perpetrated the deeds that were subsequently exposed in the court in The Hague. For the roots of ethnic cleansing in that territory we need to go back to the time when the Congo was the personal fiefdom of King Leopold II of the Belgians (from 1885). During his sovereign control of a territory which included modern-day Rwanda, a mercenary army was used to enforce labour in an economic system that resulted in a genocide whose magnitude cannot be determined. Estimates vary between five and ten million people. The record is blurred because the files relating to King Leopold's rule were destroyed when the territory was transferred to the Belgian government in 1908.

But why, following independence, was the Congo torn apart by civil wars in which an estimated four million people have died? To attribute deaths on this scale to crude notions of inter-tribal animosity is to gloss over the dynamics of a history that programmed the systematic slaughter of innocent people. To understand the current plight of indigenous peoples we need to clarify the cultural consequences of the way in which European nations grabbed other people's natural resources.

As we have noted, land tenure was one of the key organising principles of traditional cultures. If you disturb people's rights to land, shock waves are sent all the way through the psychology of the individual to the sociology of the extended family, coursing deep into the institutions of the community. Without this understanding, the crises of today become unintelligible.

When it comes to naked terror, few cases can compete with the genocide in the central African republic of Rwanda. About 800,000 people were slaughtered in 1994, the majority Tutsis massacred by Hutus. For the rest of the world, that barbarity was explained in terms of human nature and a conflict between two tribes. In fact, the route to understanding this and previous cases of genocide must be traced back to the beginning of the 20th century when Germany, followed by Belgium, intervened in the cultural affairs of these people. The facts summarised here rely on the monumental study by René Lemarchand. [12]

Africa was divided into territorial units occupied by distinct tribes. They co-existed by respecting each others claims to the right of access to land. Customs and practices were fine-tuned to both human nature and the ecological habitats which they occupied. Ancient wisdom ensured that the earliest humans could emerge to achieve the full moral and intellectual accomplishments that made it possible for the greatest of journeys in human history – the diaspora out of Africa.

In the territory that first the Germans and then the Belgians administered as Rwanda, the authority structure was built around a system of chieftains who ensured the equalisation of access to land. This guaranteed that families could procreate on the land they needed.

---

12 Lemarchand (1970).

The chiefs administered a "land tax" (*butaka*), which traditionally involved one day's labour out of five. This enabled the chiefs to make sure that the clan and tribal "infrastructure" was maintained at the level consistent with the needs of their communities.

The Belgian authorities intervened with custom and practice in ways that unleashed chaos. Lemarchand notes that Belgian intervention "spelled protracted chaos". The aloofness of the colonial administrators permitted changes that were to have fatal consequences. "The Belgians had no precise understanding of the functions ascribed to the land chief, the cattle chief and the army chief." [13] One outcome was that the chiefs decided to raise the *butaka* to two or even three days out of six. New corvées were introduced, such as the construction of houses in durable materials for the chiefs. The enterprise of the peasants was disrupted as their tribal leaders, under the patronage of colonial administrators, enriched themselves in ways that offended ancient customs.

The majority found themselves exploited by the combination of Belgian administrators and tribal leaders. True, the Europeans had introduced hospitals and built roads, but "their cost in terms of human labour, taxation and regimentation was extremely heavy. When added to customary tithes, tributes and corvees, the 'civilising' aspects of the Belgian presence made the rule of the chiefs a singularly uncivilised one". [14]

The Hutus reported that before the Europeans came "any man could go anywhere he wanted to find good soil", but "now our people must stay in one place and are beaten in order to grow certain crops". The beatings were generally administered by the Tutsis, and it was this shift in the relative powers of the two tribes that was to have a terrible impact on the population of Rwanda in the neo-colonial era.

At first, the Belgians wanted to favour the Hutus against the Tutsis. They were warned that any attempt to "eliminate the Tutsi caste" would lead to a revolution that would push "the entire state directly into anarchy and to bitter anti-European Communism". In the event, policy was reversed and the Tutsis were favoured by their colonial masters.

---

13 Lemarchand (1970: 71).
14 Lemarchand (1970: 123).

Hutu chiefs and sub-chiefs were dismissed from office and replaced by "well-born Tutsi".

This discrimination displayed itself in several ways, including educational opportunities. The Tutsis were favoured while the Hutus were excluded from the advanced education that was needed to administer communities at the level required by urbanising economies. The Belgians consolidated the right to land in favour of Tutsis, which gave them added power over the Hutus. With greater control over land, the Tutsis derived not just political advantage but also a head start in commerce in the emerging towns. The cleavage in power and authority sharpened the divide between the two tribes.

Not surprisingly, the exploited peasantry turned to home-grown prophets whom they believed could rescue them from the servitude of the corvée.

Tutsi supremacy was strengthened by three waves of changes that consolidated their standing: (i) territorial expansion of Tutsi political power; (ii) rigorous control over all educational opportunities; and (iii) the introduction of legal machinery designed to perpetuate the subjugation of the Hutu caste.

Here was the classic colonial strategy of divide-and-rule in action. The parachuting of Tutsi chiefs into predominantly Hutu areas began under the German protectorate but was refined by the Belgians, and even after the Second World War "the consensus of opinion among Belgian administrators was that the Tutsi should remain the sole recipients of secular and missionary education".[15]

The unbalanced "growth" of these societies did not occur by accident. It was the result of a colonial dynamic. The rapacious appropriation of other people's natural wealth could not be engineered without "pacifying the natives". Future generations paid the price. Given the intense feelings of fear and envy that erupt within such dislocated, dysfunctional territories, it is not surprising that terror tactics would one day be revived in the neo-colonial period. In the case of Rwanda, that terror did not surface in Antwerp, the city to which the wealth of that country had been exported. Instead, the terror was turned within,

---

15 Lemarchand (1970: 74).

resulting in the genocidal butchery of whole communities. The Tutsis had been tutored to believe that they were superior to the Hutu majority. In taking out the machetes to assert their dominance, they were playing out in the most primitive of ways the rule, noted by Lemarchand, that "in Rwanda, as in many other societies in Africa, control over the land was traditionally linked to the exercise of political rights".[16] By failing to calibrate land rights to serve the cause of freedom, the Belgians and Tutsi chiefs transformed the hierarchy of politics in a way that would one day lead to the mass burial of innocent victims in graves along the dirt roads of Rwanda.

British investigator E.D. Morel, a century ago, was shocked by what was done to Africans in the name of the King of the Belgians. Europeans were responsible for inhumanitarian behaviour in the Congo "to supply King Leopold and his financiers with revenues, and his soldiers and their crowd of retainers with food stuffs".[17] Morel recognised that the problem behind such horrors was the abuse of the primacy of one's right to land and labour.

One British imperial civil servant (Sir Harry Johnston) noted that the Belgian king sanctioned a brutal regime designed to enrich himself at the expense of the indigenous peoples. Sir Harry himself confessed that he had played his part in reshaping tribal cultures by instituting "a Hut Tax in regions entrusted to my administration; that I have created Crown Lands which have become the property of the Government; that as an agent of that Government I have sold and leased portions of African soil to European traders..."[18]

When the British compiled their Parliamentary indictment of the Belgians in the Congo in 1905, Sir Harry stressed that a better way did exist. It included taxation of a kind that need not be oppressive. The clue to the sensible social contract was contained in this proposal:

> But the Crown Lands, the public forests, the natural resources of the Congo Free State instead of being administered as a natural fund for the maintenance and improvement of that

---

16   Lemarchand (1970: 130).
17   Morel (2005: 73-74).
18   Sir Harry Johnston, Introduction to Morel (2005: xiv).

State, and the promotion of the welfare of its inhabitants, are actually diverted to the private profit of King Leopold and some of his associates. *It is this that is the inherently false principle in the scheme of the Congo Free State.* The public revenues collected from these regions are not publicly accounted for.[19]

The Congo was a classic colonial land grab in which black and white failed to develop a model for co-existence that would be to the mutual benefit of everyone. That lesson has not been learnt even to this day.

---

19 Morel (2005: xvi). Emphasis in the original

Part 3
Structures of Violence

AFTER joining the League of Nations the Abyssinians were told they must abandon slavery altogether. When ordered by the Emperor they promptly released 10,000. But the slaves owned no land and consequently had no means of earning a living. They did not know where to go or what to do and promptly went back to their old masters. A short while ago I was told that the Abyssinians were willing to free all their slaves, but when I was there they were still waiting for the League to explain what to do with them when they were freed.
– Victor Heiser, M.D., "An American Doctor's Odyssey"
(Land & Freedom, Jan-Feb 1937)

Chapter 7

Neo-colonialism & the Dysfunctional State

MANY former colonial territories have turned into failed states. Responsibility is generally placed on post-independence leaders. While not wishing to exonerate them for their failures, a full assessment is needed if appropriate remedial policies are to be formulated. We shall examine countries in three continents – Guyana, Zimbabwe and Afghanistan – to isolate the issues common to these cases of political instability.

Following Guyana's independence in 1966, race riots and deaths fostered the notion that Africans and Indians could not co-exist. But what denied such a small population, occupying 83,000 sq. miles, peaceful co-existence? Treating the civil disturbances as racially based served to camouflage the fact that the people were locked into a dispute over land.

> This is essentially an issue of land. Blacks in Guyana have been reluctant to work the land largely because of the painful historical connotation. Many still relate the land to their suffering as slaves and therefore apportion lower status to those who work on it today. The Indians, who came to the country as indentured labourers, had no such qualms. Many have since bought large tracts of land which they now farm successfully.[1]

---

1 August (1983).

But how does this account for the failure of politics?

The power, transport and communications infrastructure was dilapidated, in a country rich in gold, bauxite and precious stones. Was it psychological indoctrination, or political adventurism, that drove the politicians to Marxism? Or was the social chaos the consequence of economic policies pursued in the 19th century? Guy Standing, a senior economist at the International Labour Organisation in Geneva, analysed the issues.

Since acquiring the territory before the abolition of slavery in 1838, economic policy was focused on what Standing called "contrived stagnation".[2] The territory wedged between Brazil and Venezuela had produced a wide variety of crops, with the potential for a diversified manufacturing sector based on timber. But the British plantation owners, backed by the colonial government, eliminated that diversity in favour of monoculture (sugar) and the extraction of bauxite.

Landowners wanted to hold wages down while retaining workers on their plantations. They imported slaves until this practice was outlawed, and then imported indentured workers from the Indian sub-continent. But once the Indians had served out their indentures they were free agents. And the offspring of slaves were also free to work for themselves. How could they be prevented from settling on the vast virgin hinterlands of a country the size of Britain? Legal devices were used to force them back to the coast to work on the sugar plantations and down the bauxite mines.

The plantocracy secured low labour costs by deliberately being inefficient in the use of land, and by building an increasingly monopolistic structure for the cane industry. At all costs, people had to be prevented from saving money, because capital accumulation among the labouring population "would have developed a sector in direct competition with the estates for labour power, which would have led to greater labour shortage on the estates and higher wage rates".[3]

The concentration of land into fewer hands is measured by the number of estates. Sugar plantations shrank from 308 at the time of

---
2 Standing (1978).
3 Standing (1978: 52).

Emancipation in 1838 to 105 in 1884, 46 (1904), 21 (1949), down to two multi-nationals in 1975 when the industry was nationalised. Between 40% and 50% of land on the plantations was kept idle and beyond the reach of peasants.

The artificial scarcity of land was aided by the fact that the hinterland was designated as Crown land. This enabled the colonial government to suppress attempts by people to create their own communities. The first attempt was made in the 1840s by ex-slaves who purchased land collectively (often abandoned estates) in what became known as the village movement.

> To retain control over the labouring population and create an impoverished peasantry the estates and colonial officials had to destroy these initiatives, and the means by which they did so had a lasting effect on the underdevelopment of the Guyanese economy.[4]

To deter settlement, the price of Crown land was fixed above its market value. By the 1860s the price of Crown land was set at about five times the prices fetched by land elsewhere in Guyana.

The second attempt at creating settlements was made by what became known as the creek and river movement. The authorities killed this project by sending raiding parties to burn stores and ruin crops.

> The interior was not and never has been extensively settled, and the great majority of the population were forced to live near the estates on fragmented landholdings that were insufficient to provide more than the very barest of subsistence incomes. Faced with additional demands, such as rent and taxes, and a continuing inability to develop the infrastructure essential for productive land utilisation… the peasantry faced a stagnation that was truly contrived and became dependent on wage employment to raise an adequate subsistence income.[5]

---

4 Standing (1978: 54.
5 Standing (1978: 55).

The colonial government harassed the peasants with legislation and ordinances that prevented them from developing their own farms. By channelling workers back on to the sugar plantations, wages were curbed and rents maximised.

Thus, the British subverted patterns of land used and population dispersal that would have been efficient. In aid of this project of exploitation, the colonial authorities declined to develop property laws that secured titles to land. Peasants could not borrow money without those titles, and the machinery for land registration was not in place. Guy Standing observes: "It is not being too conspiratorial to assert that this was deliberate".[6]

At the end of the 19th century, commercial groups began to exert their pressure. Their interests, unlike the plantocracy, were best served by increases in production. And so, in 1897, a Tax Ordinance was passed which imposed a charge on "ruinate" land so as to stimulate production and terminate claims to land by those without title. Such a charge, modest though it was, would have given a gentle push in the direction of efficiency and economic growth. But the government failed to set up the machinery for collecting the tax, which was repealed in 1900.

Thus, the inertia of government with respect to its obligations to establish efficient revenue policies, and its prejudice against independent economic enterprise, laid the foundations for economic stagnation and a culture of discontent. This consequently disposed the population towards post-colonial socialism. In a country that once exported cotton, coffee and cocoa, the legacy of colonial rule was a crude economy and widespread malnutrition. Politics was biased against a diversified cash economy in favour of the rent-seeking plantation owners for whom competition was anathema.

The vulgarity of official policy is incredible – unless, of course, one locates policy in terms of discrimination and exploitation. Thus, despite the malnutrition, at one point the authorities even outlawed the production of rice. And those peasants who grew cane were forced to sell their crops to plantation owners at below market prices.

---

6 Standing (1978: 58).

Both Africans and Indians were in the vice-like grip of a doctrine that created an artificial scarcity of land and then caned them with damaging taxes.

> Government fiscal policy was traditionally highly regressive, channelling funds from the labouring population to the estates and latterly to urban areas; it also penalised many poorer productive groups by its tariff policies.[7]

The centralisation of economic and political power in the hands of monopolists and the bureaucracy laid the foundations for the nationalisation of the means of production and the centralised power of the Marxist state in the post-colonial era. But the communist model was also inefficient and could not be sustained indefinitely. It broke down in the 1980s with the coming to power of Desmond Hoyte as President. He warned that there would be "purgatory before paradise". The people of Guyana have certainly been through purgatory, but they continue to wait for a taste of paradise.

Zimbabwe: the Heartsick

IN OTHER colonial territories, socialism was the only doctrine on offer to freedom fighters. But for Rhodesia, the socialist state was *not* the only choice. The people were offered a viable alternative.

The roots of this territory's tragedy have to be traced back to the arrival of the Pioneer Column of white adventurers searching for gold in Mashonaland in 1890. The displacement of the Shona is described by Martin Meredith.

> The scramble for land in the 1890s became little more than plunder. Farms were pegged out regardless of whether local people were living there. Initially Cecil Rhodes promised each of the 200 pioneers free farms of 1,500 morgen (3,175 acres). But a host of fortune-hunters – quasai-aristocrats,

---

7 Standing (1978: 71).

military men, and speculators – followed in the wake, grabbing land at every opportunity.[8]

Ninety years later, with independence, the ownership of land was heavily skewed in favour of the white settlers (Table 8:1).

Speculators had staked their biggest claims in the high veldt of Mashonaland and Matabeleland, which included a large part of the most fertile territory. Disease and a shortage of labour, however, meant that many farms were left idle. The first uprisings took place in 1896. But Britain, by right of conquest, would not yield. Native reserves were created on which to herd "traditional" communities. The whites continued to encroach on black territories. In the 1930s, as the settlers drove the indigenous people off their homelands, about 7m acres of the land which they held within 35 miles of the railway line was left vacant.[9]

Under the Land Apportionment Act, the black population of 1m in 1931 was allocated 29m acres. The white population of 48,000 (with 11,000 actually settled on the land) held 48m acres. The expulsion of Africans from white areas and into overcrowded reserves continued through to the 1960s. In one notorious case, the Tangwena refused to move from the land which had been sold from under them by Rhodes's British South African Company in 1905. In 1969, Ian Smith's Rhodesian Front government sent in the security forces to burn down their homes, destroy their crops, impound their cattle and close down the school. The chief, watching the destruction of his community, voiced the trauma of his tribe.

Table 8:1   Zimbabwe: Distribution of Land (1980)

Farmer by Type	Numbers	Percent of Land
White large-scale commercial	6,000	39
Black small-scale commercial	8,000	4
National Parks/State Forests		16

---

8   Meredith (2007: p. 112).
9   Meredith (2007: p. 114).

> It is the Europeans who have come to disturb us, to destroy our property, to deprive us of the wealth of this land. This is unforgivable. My people are heartsick. These cattle that they are driving away…they are trying to provoke my people, so that they may shoot us with their guns, because we are defenceless.[10]

And so began the war for liberation. Robert Mugabe, the Marxist freedom fighter, promised that every African would be given land once the whites were defeated. But during the peace negotiations in London, under the Lancaster House Agreement, the whites succeeded in entrenching their land rights in a Bill of Rights. Mugabe was forced to accept that redistribution would only occur if white owners were willing to sell their land at market prices. The UK agreed to provide funds for the buy-out, but these were insufficient to meet the need of a dispossessed population. Even so, much of the land that was allocated to new owners went to a new breed of elite politicians and civil servants. And despite the land hunger among the black population, "little of it was put to productive use".[11]

The alternative approach to reordering people's relationship with the land was offered by Joshua Nkomo, the larger-than-life leader who wanted to merge the market economy with a tenure that embodied the traditional wisdom of the tribes.

> We don't believe in trading land or selling land – no. And in any government that I lead, you can be certain those practices must go. That does not mean we will be taking people's land. It means that other people who haven't got money will have a chance to use land, which is the common property of everybody. And if they have to pay some rates or rents, that will go to a general fund of the people. In this way citizens can use as much land as they want. Our system is this: once you use land, that land belongs to you. But you

---

10 Meredith (2007: p 117).
11 Meredith (2007: p. 121).

have not bought it. You cannot sell it to someone. The land belongs to the people, but everything on that land is yours.

This model would have effected a smooth transfer of power and production to benefit everyone.

But Mugabe would not share power with his political rival. After humiliating and excluding Nkomo from government, Mugabe despatched a crack army brigade (trained by the North Koreans) to Matabeleland, an Nkomo political stronghold. Massacres occurred as Mugabe sought to establish a one-party state. Over a period of four years, an estimated 10,000 civilians were murdered.[12]

That the opposition groups in colonial territories should align themselves with socialist doctrines is understandable. This placed the freedom fighters in opposition to colonial masters and provided the ideological means for mobilising support. But the socialist creed was abandoned in the post-colonial phase in response to the economic realities bequeathed by the retreating European powers.

Mugabe played the racist card, with increasingly hysterical denunciations of white citizens. But he was embarrassed by newspaper revelations that scores of government-owned farms intended for cultivators had been allocated to ministers and senior officials. Britain, after spending £44m on land re-settlement, cut off further support. As unemployment mounted, Mugabe isolated himself from the people whom he claimed to have liberated. And so, the model he had used to consolidate his power was repeated when he was defeated in the elections of 2008. Mugabe resurrected his ruthless techniques for securing quiescence, by expelling the people of the slums in Harare and applying terror tactics against the opposition Movement for Democratic Change (MDC).

Mugabe refused to accept the verdict of the people of Zimbabwe. Forced to contest a run-off election with the opposition candidate, his henchmen killed and terrorised people who supported the MDC, whose leader, Morgan Tsvangerai, was forced to seek sanctuary in the Dutch Embassy.

---

12 Meredith (2007: p. 75).

An estimated 85 supporters of the MDC were murdered in the weeks leading up to the election of 2008, hundreds were wounded and tens of thousands displaced. All because Britain and the people fighting for freedom had failed to negotiate a post-colonial land settlement that could fulfil everyone's needs.

The United Nations Security Council condemned the Mugabe regime after a UN official reported a "staggering degree of violence" perpetrated by state agencies, war veterans and youth militias. Lord Ashdown, the former European Union High Representative for Bosnia, warned that there was a risk of genocide in Zimbabwe and that military intervention might have to be contemplated.[13] But by itself, punitive violence to unseat President Mugabe would merely preserve the terms of violence in a country that had suffered the displacement of more than 3m people as a result of the failure to resolve the land question.

Afghanistan & Fundamentalism

AFGHANISTAN entered the modern era with the formation of the Durrani Empire in 1747, but the current borders were not finally established until Britain made a bid for the territory. The first Anglo-Afghan war was fought in 1839-42. There was a further outbreak of military conflict between 1878 and 1890, before the British were finally expelled in 1919.

During the 20th century, Afghanistan became one of the pieces on the geo-political chequer board, fought over by the USSR and the USA as part of the struggle over the oil fields of the Persian Gulf. Caught in the middle of the conflict between the Great Powers were the Afghan communities, and out of this chaos emerged the warlordism that corrupted communities from within. This was the context of social instability that nurtured fanatical political-religious views that eventually surfaced as the Taliban, which seized power in 1996.

The colonial powers were "rent-seeking". The country was not only strategically located at the crossroads between East and West: it is rich in copper, zinc and iron ore in the central areas, precious and semi-precious stones such as lapis, emerald and azure in the north and east,

---

13 Evans and Philp (2008).

and there may be oil and gas reserves in the north. But these mineral resources remain largely untapped. The military campaigns distracted both the Afghan population and their foreign rulers.

The Soviet invasion and occupation (1979-1989) resulted from a rebellion that was rooted in the civil discontent that arose from the administration of the People's Democratic Party of Afghanistan (PDPA). Ceilings were placed on landholdings in an attempt to overcome some of the gross inequalities. Land was redistributed without payment of compensation and mortgages of more than five years debts were cancelled. The rebellion was the excuse which Moscow needed to try and control the territory for its geo-political purposes.

But the internal turmoil must be traced to the failure of policy on land use rather than the East-West machinations. A thorough study by Liz Wily reached this conclusion:

> Long years of misdirected policy have entrenched, rather than improved, deeply inequitable and often unjust land ownership relations among tribes, between agricultural and pastoral systems and among feudally-arranged classes of society. Attempts to remedy these have been poorly executed. Violence, insecurity, anarchy and land grabbing compound these problems.[14]

Wily concludes that landlessness in the rural areas was around 43% in the 1960s and 30% in the 1990s. In 1967, 42% of the land was owned by 2.2% of farmers. Despite the subsequent attempts to redistribute land, in 2002, 2.2% owned nearly 19% of the total area. The regional variations were enormous to the point where national averages are almost meaningless. But Wily had no doubt that there was a clear correlation between political power, personal prosperity and access to land.

When the Taliban exploited the civil and economic chaos to take control of Afghanistan in 1996, "inter-factional fighting and land-grabbing continued as individuals and groups gained and lost power".[15]

---

14 Wily (2003: 5).
15 Wily (2003: 49).

The subsequent overthrow of the Taliban regime by the US did not lead to a comprehensive land policy. Instead, policy focused on the registration of titles to private land to facilitate the use of this asset as collateral for loans from banks. This was consistent with the Western model of land tenure, but previous attempts at Western-style land reform have ended in tears. So the grief suffered by the people of Afghanistan as the price paid to render it safe from terrorists may fail if land policy is not correctly framed to re-unite the population. As Wily warns us:

> Land tenure issues have been a catalyst to the social and political disquiet in Afghanistan of the last century, helping to trigger local conflict, rebellion, disorder, civil war and even foreign occupation.[16]

The failure of policy offers rich rewards for the unscrupulous for, as Wily notes, "Land (and related control over water) remains the ultimate booty in the agrarian state".[17] The lesson is clear. If the US/UK alliance fighting in Afghanistan at the beginning of the 21st century really wants to deliver peace, it ought to give priority to exploring the strengths and weaknesses of previous attempts at land reform. And that policy is more complex than merely conducting a cadastral survey to help bankers who want to lend money in the form of mortgages.

> Just as *land policy* and land law have become integral elements of state making, *the right to land* has been continually buffeted back and forth in the yet unfinished game of nation building. Tenure insecurity has been the constantly re-visited casualty.[18]

Even without good data, it is possible to conclude that there has been an increase in polarisation in the distribution of land following the Soviet invasion. Holdings have been fragmented and assets stripped

---

16 Wily (2003: 61).
17 Wily (2003: 62).
18 Wily (2003: 62). Emphasis in the original.

by the elites. The destitution associated with landlessness will intensify the challenges of governance. Some observers claim that the welfare of Afghan citizens is now of less concern to the authorities in Kabul, and their American patrons, than the interests of foreign investors.

Not everyone loses as a result of conflict. The urban land market in Kabul, for example, is very active, with land prices rising steeply to the point where officials have complained that local families are not able to afford housing.

Complaints that there is not enough land to buy in rural areas complement the overheated urban land market. The economic stress for peasants arising from the failure of land policy has serious consequences for Europe. Peasants have set aside their food-growing activities in favour of cultivating poppies. The CIA estimates that one-third of the country's GDP comes from opium exports.

The use of countervailing force by the West to combat the export of violence by failed states has not worked. The need is for a reconciliation between the rich countries and their former client states. But this will not happen if statesmen continue with the state of denial. For example, the Anglo-American coalition that launched its assault on Iraq denies that it was driven by the quest for oil rents. But Alan Greenspan, the former chairman of America's central bank (the Federal Reserve), who was an insider in the Washington power structure, broke ranks to expose that lie. In his memoirs, referring to the Bush/Blair attack on Iraq in 2004, he states: "I am saddened that it is politically inconvenient to acknowledge what everyone knows: the Iraq war is largely about oil".[19]

The rents of nature's resources were the magnet that attracted the European powers in the colonial era. Could they become the source of a new settlement for global peace in the 21st century?

---

19 Greenspan (2007: 463).

Chapter 8

Fascism:
Italy's Fourth Shore

FASCISM originates from a pathologically disturbed relationship between a population and its living space.

Hitler's Nazi regime was animated by the concept of *lebensraum* – living space. Like the household economy that evolved into the Mafia, fascism also emerged because of the failed nature of the state within which it was incubated. Historically speaking, Mussolini preceded Hitler, so we shall focus on the Italian case.

Italy was a latecomer in the history of European state formation (1861). This placed it at a disadvantage. Britain, France and other states had long since launched their colonial projects. Italy's unification might have succeeded if it had been grounded in policies of statesmanship. The alternative to hot metal penetrating flesh and blood is a matrix of tenure-and-tax policies:

- tenure of the land that secures for the population the personal freedoms that lead to the renewal of culture.
And
- taxation that secures the liberty of each person to work, save and invest in the future of themselves, their families and their communities.

The people of the peninsula were provided with neither of these policies. Instead, unification delivered "Patria" – and the right to emigrate to the

USA. Then, discouraged by America's Depression of the 1930s, Italians turned to fascist nationalism – and the right to emigrate to Africa. Finally, after defeat in the second world war, Italians worked for the unification of Europe – and the right to emigrate to Paris and Düsseldorf.

The failures of statesmanship had to be resolved at the expense of other people. In the summer of 1911, Europe turned its attention to colonial prospects on the African continent. Germany, desperate to catch up with her rivals, struck in Morocco. This led to the Franco-German agreement, in which Morocco was conceded to France and Germany received a small portion of the Congo. Italy was excluded. National pride dictated the need to stake a claim to imperial status. With the new scramble for Africa, Italy decided to bid for fringes of the Ottoman Empire: Tripolitania and Cyrenaica, the two major regions of what would become Libya.

The posturing, power-hungry Benito Mussolini stepped onto the world stage on October 28, 1922, when he grabbed power in Rome. Previously, he had denounced the Italian authorities in strident Marxist terms. On the invasion of North Africa, he proclaimed that

> Every honest socialist must disapprove of this Libyan adventure, it means only useless and stupid bloodshed.[1]

In years to come, Mussolini mobilised racist theory and statist power to decimate the Bedouin tribes of North Africa in a way that was hardly compatible with the sentiments of "honest socialists". But by then he was at the head of a failing capitalist state. Libya was a safety valve where he could put his doctrines to the test.

After the Second World War, John Wright, a British journalist working in Tripoli, investigated the impact of the Italians during the period of conquest. He combed the official documents in Rome, and reached this assessment of Mussolini's tactics:

- The conquest of all Libya was almost a sacred duty if Fascism was really to be the 'education for combat' that Mussolini

---

1 Cited in Wright (1969: 128).

intended. The Libyan war of 1922-32 was good propaganda material for militant Fascism both in Italy and abroad, but only in the last stages of the war were there signs of the flaunted ruthlessness, and even of the desire to shock international opinion, that later characterised the conquest of Ethiopia.[2]

Stripped of its pompous theorising, fascism was a melange of doctrines about racial superiority that could be used to camouflage the failings of a state that had institutionalised poverty on a grand scale for centuries. This failure was to cost the lives of at least 500,000 Libyans who died in battle, or from disease, starvation or thirst. In addition, 250,000 Libyans were expelled into exile in neighbouring countries.[3]

The nomadic and pastoral lifestyle of the peoples of Tripolitania and Cyrenaica – the two regions separated by a desert that ran all the way up to the Mediterranean shore – was the product of the desert ecology. Just 5% of the country was suitable for cultivation. Geography and politics were integrated by an ecology divided into the regions of the coast, the plain and the mountains. Historically, water and land were owned collectively by tribes, with mobility and militarism providing the social dynamic to ensure the continuity of economic activity and defence of the tribal homeland. Over the centuries, the population remained stable. By 1911 it was estimated at between 1m and 1.5m inhabitants.[4]

Under the Ottoman Empire, land was divided into five categories: privately owned, state, religious endowment land, "no man's land" and "dead" land. Libya did not have a large land-owning class until the Ottoman Land Code of 1858, which was intended to raise the efficiency of tax collecting. The registration of land led to the emergence of some families whose prominence was associated with their claim to land. As a result of the Tax Code, "the family consequently became more important than the tribe".[5]

Thus, by the time the Italians decided that they had a superior claim to Libya than the tribes, an ecologically efficient social system

---

2 Wright (1969: 153).
3 Ahmida (1994: 1).
4 Ahmida (1994: 15).
5 Ahmida (1994: 37).

existed, having survived in arid conditions for at least a thousand years. Ahmida's account of social relationships corrects the Eurocentric histories of Africa by analysing the interaction between ecology, production and land tenure.[6]

Mussolini did not respect other people's past. He identified Italy's mission in Libya in these terms: "Civilisation, in fact, is what Italy is creating on the Fourth Shore of our sea; Western civilisation in general and Fascist civilisation in particular".[7] He claimed to be building something new out of the ashes of a failed social system that had apparently left the leaders of Italy with no option but to order the grab of other people's land. According to Mussolini, the empire which he was aiming to create (and founded in 1937) was "not only a territorial, military and mercantile expression, but a spiritual and moral one".[8]

Back in 1912, Italy coveted Tripolitania and Cyrenaica for two reasons. First, it wanted to make sure that other European states could not colonise the land immediately opposite its shores on the other side of the Mediterranean. Second, Italy needed to relocate its landless peasants. It took two military campaigns to achieve this objective. In doing so, the Italians decimated the Bedouin population by half to two thirds by death and emigration between 1911 and 1932.[9] Exact numbers are not known, but it was not just a case of killing the indigenous population; the Italians were also determined to destroy the cultural base on which the Bedouin relied for their livelihoods.

Cultural Genocide

THE TRAGEDY that befell the Arab tribes was chronicled by a distinguished anthropologist from the University of Oxford. Professor E.E. Evans-Pritchard was present during the Second World War as the Bedouin sided with the British army in their attempt to expel the Italians. His field work resulted in *The Sanusi of Cyrenaica*.

Evans-Pritchard was disgusted at the maltreatment of the people of the desert, who were out-gunned by the modern weaponry of

---

6 Ahmida (1994: 6).
7 Quoted in Wright (1969: 169).
8 Wright (1969: 181).
9 Evans-Pritchard (1949: 191).

the Europeans. But the Italians, in their rush to relive the glories of the ancient Roman empire, employed psychological and cultural terrorism as well as military hardware to undermine the shifting communities that had evolved in sympathy with the arid deserts and mountains.

On their arrival, the Italians found that the tribes were loosely linked by an Order of Sufis known as the Sanusiya. They were orthodox Muslims from the Sunni strand of Islam. The Fascists determined that, if the Bedouin rebels were to be demoralised, their religious faith would have to be destroyed. The Sanusi would have to be demolished, and "The confiscation of the estates of the Order was viewed as the final act in its extirpation". The Italian authorities had originally assured the Order that the customs of the people would be respected. But, Evans-Pritchard noted, they spoke in bad faith; for they had secured popular support for their war "among the peasants of Southern Italy by promising them the exploitation of an Eldorado in Libya".[10] So, "as soon as the Italians had been powerful enough to seize the endowments of the Order they had seized them. Their action can only be called theft. It was a violation of the Shari'a law, repeatedly proclaimed inviolable by the Italians".[11]

When Mussolini grabbed power in 1922, he abandoned his socialist sentiments.

> The Fascists felt that their prestige was at stake. The days of *socialdemocratzia* were over and military conquest, domination, and colonisation were the order of the day. The ancient Roman provinces were once again to be peopled by the sons and daughters of Rome[12]

By eliminating the Sanusiya, the Bedouins would be deprived of their leaders. But undermining their spiritual life was not sufficient.

---

10 Evans-Pritchard (1949: 192).
11 Evans-Pritchard (1949: 195).
12 Evans-Pritchard (1949: 156).

- The people had to be brutalised psychologically. The Italians spoke of them as "barbarians, little better than beasts, and treated them accordingly".[13]
- Survivors had to be mentally and physically refashioned as peasant-tenants of the state and wage-labourers. They were prosecuted for retaining their Bedouin lifestyle, which in any case became increasingly impossible as the Italians appropriated their land.
- The tribal sheikhs had to be humiliated: they were a cornerstone of social organisation, and their authority was accordingly undermined.

In schools, Arab children were forced to replace their native language with Italian; and adults were directed to menial work. This transformation of personality was a price worth paying, as far as Mussolini was concerned. For as he wrote in his entry in the *EnciclopediaItaliana*:

> [F]or the Fascist, everything is in the State, and nothing human or spiritual exists, much less has value, outside the state.[14]

The African colonies of other European powers were transformed over a period of 80 years, but the Italians took less than half of that time to redesign their provinces. In the early 1920s, Italy had registered its claim to over 120,000 hectares, but within the next few years they appropriated 450,000 hectares. There was a measure of compensation, but as Evans-Pritchard noted: "[I]n order to make it look a little less like common robbery it was decided to make a parade of indemnification".[15]

To display his macho credentials to other powers, Mussolini crucified a way of life that had sustained people in the centuries after the last traces of the Holy Roman Empire were erased by sand storms. He did not want to invest Italian capital on Libyan soil, to provide work

---

13 Evans-Pritchard (1949: 196).
14 Cited in Evans-Pritchard (1949: 208).
15 Evans-Pritchard (1949: 223).

for Arabs. He wanted a resettlement programme for landless Italians who would work their own farms, so that they could export to the fatherland the products that were expensive to import from other countries.

Removing the existing users of the soil was executed with Fascist ruthlessness, leaving whole regions "sad, ruinous, and depopulated". Wright observed:

> Villages and markets were dead, and the flocks and herds that represented the main wealth of the people had been decimated by war and drought; there were 800,000 sheep in Cyrenaica in 1926; in 1933 there were less than 100,000; the camel population had dropped from 75,000 to 2,600, horses had been reduced from 4,000 to 1,000. After their experience of [Colonel Rodolfo] Graziani's concentration camps, the nomads were sullen, frightened, and destitute.[16]

Between 1926 and 1929, 160,000 acres were set aside for sale on 10-year mortgages. The process was stepped up in the early 1930s, with four model villages constructed in Cyrenaica. Fifty-acre farms were made available to 150 hand-picked families from the poverty-stricken region of Puglia, in southern Italy. This was followed by mass settlement of peasant colonists in Tripolitania. Guiding the colonisation was the official slogan "Believe, Obey, Fight". Preparations to receive 20,000 colonists were made in 1938, with model farms, roads and villages completed with "Fascist speed".

> To desperately poor, and mainly landless, peasants the offer of a new life in Libya, no matter how hard, seemed to be another of the Duce's miracles.[17]

The Tripoli and Benghazi streets welcomed the settlers with banners proclaiming "Mussolini redeems the soil and founds cities". Farms

---

16 Wright (1969: 177).
17 Wright (1969: 173).

ranged from 37 to 124 acres, depending on the quality of the soil. Without the Second World War the "demographic colonisation" would have seen the relocation of 100,000 settlers on African soil by 1942, and 500,000 by the early 1960s. But even these numbers would not have relieved the pressure on the plight of the unemployed in Italy, for "the natural increase in population was greater than the greatest possible flow of migrants to the Fourth Shore".[18]

Reconciliation: Reckoning with Islam

THE US Government, regarded him as one of the most notorious of leader outlaws, a pariah beyond the pale of international law. But the seeds of the Gaddafi dictatorship were sown by the Italian colonists.

Col. Muammar Gaddafi did seize power in a coup, but his "terrorist" state was not the product of the perverse psychology of a band of power-hungry soldiers. To understand the emergence of the Islamic faith as a factor in 21st century geo-politics, we need to take account of the dynamics of colonial land grabs.

The tribes of the Libyan hinterland had resisted both the Ottoman and colonial states through to the mid-1930s because they had access to "free land" – the desert. This provided security and sustenance during unstable times, enabling the nomads to continue their pastoralism over the centuries. Ali Abdullatif Ahmida records early colonial contact and notes:

> Sufi Islam, tribal military organisation, and oral traditions were crucial cultural and social weapons in the fight against colonialism…The displacement of the Ottoman empire by Italian colonialism renewed the need for tribal-peasant confederations as governing centers and thus explains their dominance over social life even after independence in 1951… The modern Libyan nation-state is a recent construction, a product of the colonial period and the reaction to its impact.[19]

---

18 Wright (1969: 175).
19 Ahmida (1994: 5-7).

Despite the resilience of the tribal organisation – founded on the collective ownership of the land – the Italians overcame resistance by the early 1930s through the deployment of overwhelming fire power. But this created legendary heroes and martyrs which animated people's commitment to their faith.

> [T]hose active in the resistance emphasised an anti-colonial culture, which led to a conservative reaction in the revival of strong attachments to Islam and the clan. In other words, Islam and nationalism became synonymous. Anti-colonial Islam had its roots in popular culture and this brand of Islam became a defining element of the post-colonial Libyan state.[20]

Following independence, the attempt to create a legitimate monarchy based on the role of King Idris and family failed to secure the support of the population. In 1969 the young officers mobilised by Gaddafi drew on a radical Islamic faith to entrench their power, and Gaddafi employed anti-colonial slogans to reinforce his legitimacy. While these competing groups manipulated social history to their ends, "the essential point is that Islam and anti-colonial nationalism were products of a specific history and a reflection of ordinary people's collective memory".[21] Thus, from a Western perspective, radical Islam ought to be understood not just in terms of animosity directed against American culture today, but as the expression of anger at the colonial events of the early 20th century. That history is painful. Sustainable communities were decimated. With the passage of time and the compression of enormous deprivation, the outcome was the desire for a new form of politicised organisation, the radicalised Islamic nation-state.

But Italy was not alone in fathering radical Islam. Moving westwards along the coast to Morocco, we can trace the influence of Spain and France on the Muslim world. By the end of 1925 the French *colons* had acquired nearly half a million hectares of Morocco, a possession

---

20 Ahmida (1994: 2).
21 Ahmida (1994: 2).

which they were to double before the French Protectorate ended in 1956. The impact on the indigenous peoples was devastating, with "more and more Moroccans…forced on to marginal land, either in the mountains to the less fertile parts of the plains, and transhumant tribes saw their grazing lands cut away".[22]

The techniques for destroying the tribes and their association with their natural habitats, which had been perfected in Algeria at a slightly earlier date, were replicated in Morocco. The tax regime, for example, served two purposes. One was to extract a disproportionate share of the revenue from the Moroccans. The other was to drive Moroccans into debt, which forced them to pay usurious rates of interest. "Harvests were mortgaged in advance, and Moroccans lost land when they failed."[23] And fail the harvest would, more frequently than for the French *colons*, because tribal water was diverted to land occupied by Frenchmen. The French authorities used specious arguments based on respect for Islamic law to justify the deprivation of water rights from traditional users.

A few Arabs were enriched as tribal lands that had been held on a collective basis were privatised and sold to settlers. The outcome was inevitable.

> The Moroccan population stayed poor and the countryside and cities collapsed into disorder as the country lurched towards revolution…By 1907 a large part of the Moroccan population faced starvation…Already by 1906 European protégés owned about 30% of all land within 50kms of Tangier, and French companies bought up huge areas around Casablanca. Some of the poor expressed their frustration in individual acts of violence: murders of and attacks on Europeans increased.[24]

Instead of modernising the food production sector to make the best use of labour power and raise living standards for everyone's benefit, from the 1920s French policy supported the drive to emulate the citrus

---
22 Pennell (2000: 201).
23 Pennell (2000: 198).
24 Pennell (2000: 134-135).

industry of California. This benefited *colons* exclusively, while engaging a very few wealthy Moroccan landowners. Infrastructure works were designed to employ Frenchmen, even excluding Italian and Spanish as well as Moroccan workers.

Investors as far away as Australia planned to buy land to farm sheep in Morocco. The prospects were good, according to a report of 1911, except for the problem of the Arab people, who were

> [an] indolent, lazy lot, much given to talk and little work, and they must have degenerated from former times…The native people formed the greatest obstacle in the way of rapid development of the country: they are in possession of the land in large numbers and how to get them off and turn it to the best account is…the greatest problem that will have to be solved.[25]

Thus was laid the foundations for the disintegration of tribal institutions and personal values which, a century later, would leave its mark in the form of suicide bombers. Terrorists from one town in Morocco destroyed lives and property in places as far apart as Madrid and Baghdad. The town is Tetouan, just 30 miles from a Spanish enclave. The inhabitants provided the recruits for radical Islam. US intelligence agents using DNA evidence traced at least nine men who were responsible for suicide missions in Iraq to this little town in the foothills of the Rif Mountains, and at least another 21 individuals had left the area to seek martyrdom. According to local reports, these young men had become disillusioned with the daily struggle to earn a living. They came from the narrow streets where homes had no running water, unemployment and illiteracy rates were high, and the population vulnerable to the teachings of spiritual leaders who proclaimed the virtues of murderous deeds in the name of God.

Reporter Fiona Govan questioned relatives to assemble a portrait of the conditions that alienated men in the prime of their lives. Religious leaders pointed to the region's close proximity to Europe, where the

---

25 Cited in Pennell (2000: 148).

lifestyles were beyond the reach of the jobless Moroccans who became frustrated and consequently (in some cases) attracted to martyrdom.[26]

Containing the threat of Islamic suicide bombers will not be accomplished with guns, or the "pacification" of the natives with foreign "aid" funnelled through Western corporations. If there is to be a reckoning with the faith of the Muslim world, it will need to be grounded in the good faith of the West. As yet, there is no sign of that good faith, because the source of the conflict is not allowed to intrude into the debate. The West still wants to extract rents from their land, haemorrhaging the material vitality of the Muslim world.

---

26 Govan (2006).

Chapter 9

Economics of the Covenant

GLOBALLY speaking, violence is now entrenched as politics by other means. Variants of religious fundamentalism propagated in the name of Islam, to justify human sacrifices as live bombs, is one example. Sacralizing cruelty – turning it into a sacred ritual – is effective in animating some individuals to perpetrate terrible deeds.

> This logic is uncomfortably close to that employed by terrorists: my grievances are so huge that they justify any measures I may take, even killing the innocent.[1]

Using God's name to justify violence, when God – as represented in the scriptures of all the major religions – offers the solution to injustices in the use of nature, is grotesque. But the political philosophies that govern "on the ground" fail to assure people that their rights and needs can be met. This is evident in the large parts of the world that continue to search for a post-colonial settlement. What should have been an emancipation for everyone - the transition to political sovereignty - turned into a nightmare. That is what happened with the division of the Punjab region of India into Muslim West Pakistan and the Hindu-occupied Indian Punjab. Previously, Punjabi Hindus, Sikhs and Muslims lived peacefully together. The partition resulted in 10m refugees and the death of more than 1m people in inter-communal strife.

---

1 Taylor (2009: 258).

Independence, as the peasants of India discovered, far from ending the colonial influence, proved to be a continuation of the old system by new means. Legal processes that united old colonialism with the nation-building of the last 50 years *continued the displacement of people from their land*. The underlying propensity for systemic violence continued unabated in the largest democracy in the world. This is a characteristic of most former colonies and the chief legacy of the British empire, according to, among others, historian Piers Brendon.[2]

The scale of the displacement of people in India has been partially estimated by the World Bank. About 10m people lose their homes and their economic base every year. These are the victims of just two activities that are supposed to accelerate development: investment in dams, and in urban transport.[3] In the 10 years covered by the World Bank study, an estimated 90-100m extra people were rendered landless by mega-projects funded both privately and publicly. That displacement caused untold – and consistently ignored – hardship. The sociologist who led the World Bank's taskforce, Dr. Michael Cernea, emphasises that the estimate was conservative "yet nothing less than stunning". He compared the annual 10m displaced people with the number of refugees worldwide (assessed by the UNHCR), which is put at 15-20m. But while the refugees make the TV headlines, the much larger number of people displaced by infrastructure investments are all but ignored.

> Official misunderstanding or sheer ignorance about the complex economics of displacement and recovery are simply appalling in many agencies and countries. Many pitfalls in current practice can be traced to the sorry state of the economic research on resettlement and to the flawed prescriptions for economic and financial analysis, and for planning, in this domain.[4]

---

2 Brendon (2007).
3 World Bank (1994).
4 Cernea (1996: 31).

Cernea highlighted the community-wide impact of displacements.

> Such 'elusive' disintegration processes undermine livelihoods in ways uncounted and unrecognised by planners and are among the most pervasive causes of enduring impoverishment and disempowerment.[5]

The World Bank's estimate scratches the surface of the problem. It does not include the displacement and destroyed lives resulting from investment in forest and reserve parks, mining and thermal power plants and all the other enterprises that are imperative for both environmental conservation and industrial modernisation. The march of progress is intensifying the discontent within sovereign countries which are trapped in a vicious feedback system. They are sinking deeper into debt as a minority of people get rich, with millions impoverished and vulnerable to forces unseen.

People continue to be displaced under property laws that were created by former colonial masters, which deny them full compensation for their losses and exclude them from a share in the benefits that are created by the infrastructure. An example is India's Land Acquisition Act. It was passed by the British in 1894. Using a law that was designed to grab land for the enrichment of Britain, India's government and its agencies now abuse their own people by appropriating land from farmers and fishermen without compensating them for their losses or for the costs of resettlement. No attempt is made to audit the benefits that flow from urban developments, new salt works and dams, so that the net gains from the investment in infrastructure may be shared by those who made the real sacrifices. Instead, according to Gautam Appa and Girish Patel, if the authorities find themselves with surplus lands after completion of the projects, they dispose of them at a profit. They propose:

> Careful and advanced planning is needed to determine precisely the areas of lands required, and secondly the resettlement and rehabilitation policy must include a

---

5 Cernea (1996: 22).

provision that any excess lands should be handed back to the original owners.[6]

Giving the land back is one option, but it is not a realistic solution to the problem of inherited poverty and unbalanced growth.

The goal of permanent peace and prosperity is not a utopian aspiration. It is within the realms of science and technology, and it is a moral imperative if we are to save the species that are at risk of annihilation because of the way habitats are degraded. We need a new communion within our human species; the renewal of our communities and the reintegration of people in a common space: the public space. Meeting that challenge would be all the easier once we recognise the interrelatedness between our society and the material universe.

Speaking both literally and metaphorically, we need to re-colonise Earth. This re-occupation must be executed on the basis of a set of rights that accords equal opportunity to everyone to reach his or her potential for a decent human existence. The essence of this project is the development of a new spirituality, for those who are persons of faith through a new Covenant with God and the renewal of faith; or, for the secularly committed, a new contract with nature and the community. How to achieve social settlement may be considered in terms of the conflict over the land of Jerusalem, which pits Jew and Arab against each other.

Towards the New Jerusalem

OF ALL the places where the spiritual life is trapped in violent conflict, the most tragic of all is the ancient land of Palestine.

Europe owed the Jewish people a debt that needed to be paid in a practical way, but the Arab peoples of Palestine, violently displaced to make way for the state of Israel, should not have been a part of that price.[7]

The current approach to solving the dispute over the possession of the Holy Land, however, cannot be resolved by brutal suppression or

---

6 Appa and Patel (1996: 149).
7 Pappe (2006).

firing missiles over territorial boundaries, the result of which is the death of many innocent people. An approach to resolving the injustices is needed based on the understanding of our shared humanity. To assist in this ecumenical approach to resolving conflict, we can do no better than to examine the writings of Jonathan Sacks, the Chief Rabbi of the United Hebrew Congregation of Britain and the Commonwealth. One of his books elevates him close to those whom he identifies as prophetic voices – Dietrich Bonhoeffer (Nazi Germany), Martin Luther King (civil rights America) and Desmond Tutu (apartheid South Africa). The significance of this text is partly for what it reminds us; but, equally important, for what it silently glosses over.

Sacks identifies a set of conditions that would deliver the integrated society based on respect for religious and ethnic differences. A society constructed on a covenant, he writes, "is built…on strong ideals: human dignity, freedom and an equality of human worth".[8] Dignity features powerfully in this exposition. "In covenant as the Bible understands it, each individual has significance, dignity, moral worth, the right to be heard, a voice."[9]

The cornerstone of a successful attempt to re-create society, argues Sacks, is this biblical concept of the covenant, rather than the notion of the social contract. But what was the core of that covenant? *The covenant was a land deal.*

Moses was the messenger who delivered God's message to the Hebrew tribes. The tribes were wandering in the desert, and they agreed to abide by God's commandments in return for the land which they needed on which to construct their settlements. "God makes space for human freedom and invites an entire people to become, in the rabbinic phrase 'his partners in the work of creation'".[10] That space was a specified territory, allocated for the benefit of every member of all the tribes. The covenant was between God and "all the people" – not just between God and the leaders of the tribes, or an elite class within the population.

---

8 Sacks (2007: 144).
9 Sacks (2007: 106).
10 Sacks (2007: 105).

In the history of every other known polity, first comes the territory, then, many centuries later, come the laws. In the case of the Bible, the laws precede the land. The covenant, as Philip Selznick puts it, is 'pre-political, foundational, and consensual'. The Israelites must have a social covenant before they can have a social contract.[11]

The distinction between covenant and social contract is vital. As Sacks explains, the social contract establishes a political entity – the nation state. The covenant, however, is the foundation for society, its norms and values.

The social contract came into its own following the conquests of others' territories (born out of the violence of dispossessing the land already occupied by first settlers). The covenant, however, was the basis of voluntary agreement among those who wished to create a society on the principles of non-violence.

Confining himself to the case of contemporary Britain, Sacks asserts that the doctrine of multi-culturalism has not only failed, but is creating dangerous outcomes. The doctrines currently applied in an attempt to tolerate diversity is ghettoising communities, fragmenting rather than uniting people. So the terms for the desired unity need to be re-negotiated in a way that preserves the rich diversity of creed and colour, uniting everyone in a coherent community as partners. His critique of the multi-cultural doctrine is convincing, and his retrieval of the concept of the covenant is inspired. How he uses the biblical land deal to illuminate the basis of human dignity and freedom is as powerful as one could hope for, in attempting to deepen political discourse. And yet, his application of the concept is flawed.

To enrich our understanding of the terms of the relationships between individuals, Sacks deploys three metaphors.

The Country House This model is inappropriate for Sachs' purpose. The owner may generously admit strangers and allow them to occupy some of his hundreds of empty rooms, but visitors will always remain guests. "However generous their host, he remains the host, and they

---

11 Sacks (2007:106).

are guests. It is his home, not theirs. The place belongs to someone else. That is *society as country house*."[12]

The Hotel Occupants have the freedom and equality that they could not enjoy in the country house model. They are all guests. The relationship is contractual. "There is only one problem. A hotel is where you stay, not where you belong. You feel no loyalty to a hotel…It doesn't become part of your identity."[13]

Home In this model, strangers arrive in a town. They are welcomed by the townsfolk and their civic leaders, who announce:

> "We have a patch of empty land: large enough to accommodate homes for all of you. We have bricks and building materials. We have experts here who can help you design your homes, and we will help you build them. Meanwhile we will offer you hospitality while the homes are being built. Let us do this together."[14]

Unlike the country house case, the newcomers have to build their own long-term accommodation. Unlike the hotel, they do not merely pay to occupy space. It is the process of constructing their habitat which establishes the sustainable relationships. "Not only have they made a home; they have made themselves at home, in this landscape, this setting, this place."[15] In this arrangement, people have earned their place in their new home. They have a self-respect that was not available to them as guests. The newcomers have worked together with the townsfolk in the act of building and so have become part of a team.

> In fact, when the houses are finished, the new arrivals and the people of the town celebrate together. That too is a symbolic act, a ceremony of bonding, a ritual of belonging…They have added something to the town, and the townspeople know it… That is society as the home we build together.[16]

---
12 Sacks (2007: 13).
13 Sacks (2007: 14).
14 Sacks (2007: 14).
15 Sacks (2007: 14).
16 Sacks (2007: 15).

This brings us to the one ingredient that Sacks omits from his description of how to construct a society that preserves the riches of diversity within an integrated community.

On what are the homes constructed? Sacks notes: "You can't build a life, let alone a home, without foundations".[17] But you can't have foundations without land into which to sink them. Where is the *sustainable* solution to the problem of land occupation in the Sacks exposition? It doesn't make an appearance, apart from his reference to the original covenant between God and the Jews.

By reminding ourselves of the economic basis of the country house, we appreciate why Sacks pronounces it unviable as the basis for society. This splendid structure is built on land owned by an individual who, by virtue of his ownership is necessarily in a class apart from the others. So the Sacks metaphor is important in that it characterises an historically specific system: the English aristocratic form of society following the grab of monastic land in 1536 (see Box 9:1).

We can also now identify the *strengths* of the hotel model as contract politics. But, again, Sacks overlooks the economic implications of his metaphor.

Box 9:1 Society's Safety Net

IN ENGLAND, up to the time of Henry VIII, the monastic lands funded the community's safety net. The aged, and those who fell on hard times, could rely on the monasteries for immediate support. When Henry appropriated those lands, he privatised the sacred rents and wiped out the safety net. The result has been eloquently described by the late Sir Kenneth Jupp, a judge in the English High Court for 15 years, as a perversion of justice.[1]

The vagabonds took to the highways. Communities were unglued: the social glue was washed away by the state's appropriation of the land, which was then privatised for the benefit of favoured courtiers, creating a circle that then expanded into the landowning class which dictated the terms of citizenship through its control of Parliament.

1 Jupp (1997).

---

17 Sacks (2007: 143).

In the hotel case, every resident pays a rent for the space occupied: this renders everyone equal. Or does it? Who owns the hotel? Or, put another way, who pockets the rents? What matters is the ownership of the building and all its amenities, which is a separate consideration from ownership of the parcel of land on which the building sits. The hotel constructed on land that is leased from an owner merely serves as a conduit for rents to be passed on. If the hotel is literally no more than that, a hotel, then the guests are transient and this model is not a viable community. But if the hotel is taken to represent the community, a completely different outcome emerges. In this case, the individual occupant of space enjoys the privacy of the space he monopolises, but pays rent for doing so. He has the equal use of the common spaces (lounge, lifts, recreational amenities, etc.), which is shared with everyone. But if this hotel is a private corporation which appropriates the rents, we are back to the country house model – the inequality between the host and guests.

What of the "home model" into which people are welcomed? They are offered a piece of vacant land, says Sacks. But he does not tell us the terms on which the newcomers occupy that space. Do they pay rent to a private landowner? In that case, the newcomers cannot be equals. Ultimately, they are denied the dignity of belonging, because they do not enjoy equal rights over, or to use, the landscape. If the newcomers are present on condition that they yield part of their labours to particular individuals, their presence is contingent on a contractual relationship. And that is the social contract arrangement rather than the covenant.

By failing to explore the terms of the land deal as specified by God in the Bible, Sacks ends up by offering a partial solution to the challenge of how to unite Catholic with Protestant (Northern Ireland), Muslim with Hindu (Kashmir), and the tribes competing for space in Kenya, Zimbabwe and other African countries which have suffered genocidal conflicts in the post-colonial era (such as the Hutu/Tutsi conflict in Rwanda).

Without respect for shared ownership and occupation of the space, some individuals or groups must remain outsiders; and this is not the basis for *re-creating society*.

Multi-culturalism, Sacks agrees, despite its shortcomings, was a genuine advance over the politics of exclusion and narrow nationalism. But it suffers from fatal philosophical and moral weaknesses. On the other hand, by adopting an approach that conceives of building society anew, we create a viable community.

> Unlike the country-house model, it is about *collective belonging*. In a diverse society, there should be no distinction between host and guest, majority and minorities, insiders and outsiders.[18]

The only economic basis for a society that can respect diversity is one in which the problems associated with the privatisation of the land are eliminated. There can be no identification with "place", for example – to which Sacks repeatedly refers – if that place is in the exclusive ownership of someone else.

That was the genius of the covenant into which God entered with the tribes of Israel. The deal was that the people would behave according to certain moral standards (the Ten Commandments) in return for the land that would sustain them. There was nothing contingent about the significance of God's land deal. It was not just a convenient arrangement for a rootless set of people wandering around the desert. This emerges when Sacks discusses his concept of the common good, which arises when people of different creeds and ethnicities join together to create tolerant communities. But

> There are universals. We all need food and shelter; we all need to communicate with others; we all need to make space for difference if others are to make space for us.[19]

Food and shelter: the basic material needs of each and every person, family, community. You can't meet these basic needs without land. Psychologically, self-respect needs equal access to that space. Respect

---

18   Sacks (2007: 22). Emphasis added.
19   Sacks (2007: 11).

for others starts by recognising their equal right to share in the benefits of nature.

God tried to make sure that the tribes would not contest the ownership of the land, because, as conveyed by Moses and other prophets, *He* was the owner. The basis of the administration of that land was elaborated in the Bible (e.g., Leviticus, Ch. 25). The practicalities of how to administer the covenant with God need to be adapted to the exigencies of time and place, but there can be no dispute about the primacy of ownership rights, or the universal principles on which the covenant is constructed.

Federalism & the Land Tax

THE consequences of abusing each person's equal right to land abound in our communities. What Sacks calls "the dignity of difference" is not respected because outsiders are not acknowledged as having an equal stake in the material basis of the community. In fact, under the pressures caused by differential access rights, outsiders come to be treated as barbarians, as sub-human. That's why Hitler victimised the Jews in the 1930s and the Italian state is victimising the Roma people today. But it is not just "outsiders" who are viewed with animosity. People distinguished by no more than a linguistic tradition are also liable to be regarded as competitors to the point where territorial division is considered the appropriate way to settle differences (see Box 9:2).

To resolve such disputes, the notion of "covenantal politics" introduced by Jonathan Sacks is of seminal importance.[20] It deepens the language of political discourse. It begins to resolve the contests that are tearing apart societies around the world. How can the leaders of Zimbabwe reach a lasting agreement other than on terms that solve the land question? Similarly, in Northern Ireland, Sri Lanka…in fact, there is no region in the world today without territorial disputes. Even when a political agreement or military success causes the guns to fall silent, this may prove to be only a temporary cessation of hostilities unless the underlying injustice of unequal access to land is also

---

20 Sacks (2007: 135).

> **Box 9:2 Europe Divided by Property Spoils**
>
> IN EUROPE, the contests over sharing territory have not been consigned to the past, as the civil tensions in Belgium emphasise. Belgium is a mature member of the EU, and host in Brussels to NATO and the European Commission headquarters. And yet its ethnic squabbles are reminiscent of a Third World country torn by the petty struggles of tribal warlords.
>
> Belgium is threatened with a break-up because of cultural and linguistic differences. The country is locked in a dispute over identity and territory, divided because French and Dutch speakers adopt hostile postures and demand a territorial split. During the boom years up to 2007, one cause of vexation was the dispute over who should pocket the capital gains from the residential property market in Brussels, which had prospered thanks to the investment in the high-speed rail link to London. There was also the friction caused by high taxes and the anger over the subsidies to the relatively poorer Wallonia from the prosperous region of Flanders.[1]
>
> 1 Henley (2007).

resolved. Ireland, for example, was "peaceful" from the 1920s to the 1960s, when the Provisional IRA recommenced hostilities.

Sacks argues that the Hebrew Bible deserves to be taken seriously as a political text. We may concur, except that this then obliges us *not to ignore one half of the covenant between God and the people.* God gave the land on condition that it was used according to a moral code, which included the cancellation of the personal debts of the poor and the restoration of their land every 49 years (the year of the Jubilee). That code is now flouted by all societies of all creeds. This, in turn, leads to systemic violence. A federal system of politics can be constructed that respects differences of culture and creed; providing that a fiscal tool is incorporated to share the benefits of Earth equally among everyone, without distinction.

Part 4

Healing Humanity

I believe the key to our self respect - and our legacy to the next generation - is the inclusion and reparation of the First Australians. In other words, justice. There is no mystery about what has to be done. The first step is a treaty that guarantees universal land rights and a proper share of the resources of this country.

– John Pilger

CHAPTER 10

FREEDOM THROUGH TAXATION

ACCORDING to the United Nations, there is no universal human right of access to land.[1] Whether the omission from its Declaration of Human Rights was an accident, or deliberate, remains to be determined. Here, we need to focus on the question of whether peoples' land rights can be restored. One of the Founding Fathers of America certainly thought so. Thomas Jefferson wrote in a letter to James Madison on October 28, 1785:

> The earth is given as a common stock for man to labour and live on. If, for the encouragement of industry we allow it to be appropriated, we must take care that other employment be furnished to those excluded from the appropriation. If we do not, the fundamental right to labour the earth *returns to the unemployed* (italics added).

Political practice abandoned this principle, but it continues to lurk in the interstices of Western philosophy. The consistent application of the natural rights doctrine of philosophers like John Locke would remove the blight of unemployment. For Locke acknowledged that a significant portion of value was in a strong sense the result of community action. On the basis of his labour theory of property, this value could not be privately appropriated. Society had its natural fund out of which to

---

1 Harrison (2008).

defray the expenses of the community which provided services that everyone shared.

But Western social scientists and policy-makers have forgotten how to apply this principle. To dissect the way in which Western political practice undermines the will of the people, we return to the one country that has made a conscious effort to banish the tools of organised violence: Costa Rica.

Costa Rica achieved social successes that are the envy of her neighbours. Unfortunately, she is not free of the policy errors that imbue the politics of other central American countries. This was illustrated by what happened when she agreed to the terms of foreign investors who offered to provide a railroad.

Coffee was expensive to export. It had to be shipped from the Pacific port of Puntarenas down to Cape Horn and back up to the northern hemisphere. A railway to the eastern seashore would cut the shipping time to London by almost three months. Despatched from the Caribbean port of Limón, the costs of transportation would be seriously reduced, yielding profits to be shared with the producers.

But who would fund such a massive investment in transport infrastructure? The Costa Rican authorities were left in no doubt that they had one choice only: provide incentives to private investors. The capital, apparently, was not available, so the deal would have to be in kind. That led to the single biggest policy error in the history of Costa Rica. That error *was* avoidable. For under the correct pricing mechanism, the funds to pay for the railway *were* available. It was a matter of who would lay claim to the surplus income created by the enhanced productivity generated by the railway – an income that would surface as increases in what people were willing to pay for the use of land.

When Henry Meiggs Keith contracted to build the railway in 1871, sufficient knowledge had been accumulated in France and Britain to acquaint governments with the policies they needed to turn the railway project into a self-funding investment. It was understood that, when a railway cuts the costs of production, the net gains are measured as an increase in the value of land within the catchment area of the railway.[2] Through the public purse, that value may be earmarked to fund the investment. In other words, no-one need pay for the railway – it pays for itself. But Britain had pioneered the privatisation model, the central feature of which was that land owners remained free to pocket the windfall value generated by entrepreneurs and innovating engineers. Costa Rica was not going to be allowed to depart from that financial model.

Keith negotiated a deal that would be funded, in the first instance, by investors in London. The railway was completed in 1890. But of the £3.4m capital raised to fund the project, only £1.3m reached Costa Rica. Of that, £400,000 was spent in lawyers' fees to obtain the balance.[3] Costa Rica was required to grant a 90-year lease on the railroad and hand over 800,000 acres of state land. Furthermore, Costa Rica had to exempt the land from taxation for 20 years. So the railroad *was* funded out of rents; but ownership of this social revenue was transferred to Keith and his associates.

But how could the railway's owner convert the land into rental revenue? By growing bananas. The seeds were sown for a ferocious economic model that was alien to Costa Rica.

- The Tropical Trading and Transport Company metamorphosed into the United Fruit Company, an absentee foreign-owned corporation that had no allegiance to the host government or the welfare of the population. Until 1910, banana exports were free of taxes. The rental revenue drained out of the country instead of providing the financial resources for further enriching the culture of Costa Ricans.
- Jamaican and Chinese workers who were hired to build the railroad were not allowed to migrate to the Central Valley to find employment. Thus trapped, they were landless labourers locked into the labour market and not free to negotiate decent wages. This contrasted with the peasants who worked their plots and negotiated relatively high wages when they chose

---

2 Harrison (2006a).
3 Seligson (1980: 51).

to hire out their labour during the harvest season. Jamaican and Chinese workers were boxed into the classic state of dependency, so part of the wages they would have received was pocketed by the plantation owner.

The racism that marred life in other countries on the isthmus, which was otherwise absent from Costa Rica, was severely felt by the Jamaicans who worked for the United Fruit Company. Industrial unrest scarred labour relations. The Communist Party, founded in 1931, organised the banana workers and orchestrated a major strike, the first of many to follow that were peculiarly associated with the banana plantation economy. When the company abandoned its plantations on the Atlantic coast and re-located on the Pacific side, the black workers who had formerly been prohibited from migrating were left behind to fend for themselves. The economy of the region was destroyed.[4]

This history affirms the thesis that personal freedom is inextricably bound up with land tenure and taxation. When the policies that shape these are dysfunctional, people and their communities are pauperised. Elsewhere in Costa Rica, people who worked the land were owners, and there was a surplus of free land to meet the needs of a growing population. But if the land owner is granted the power to exclude people from accessing land – as happened with the Jamaican workers – the land owning employer exercises the whip hand in setting wage rates. While the Jeffersonian model of the yeoman farmer was an ideal that did fit Costa Rica for most people, it did not do so for the imported Jamaicans and Chinese.

Marxist historians would say that this was an inevitable outcome of the history of class conflict. But the model for the alternative strategy for funding the railway was available. It had been used 30 years earlier when coffee was becoming important and the growers needed an upgraded network of roads.

In 1843 the largest coffee producers established the Sociedad Económica Itineraria to promote the construction of new highways. A link from the Central Valley to Puntarenas was built

---

4 World Bank (1993: 68).

by the private sector but funded out of a tax of 1 real per 46 kgs of coffee. "Private interest, initiative, and participation in building the country's infrastructure characterised most of the century."[5] This was a partnership between private enterprise and the state, which employed a funding policy that facilitated both economic growth and stable social relationships.

The major highway to the coast, completed in 1846, made it possible to increase production in new areas along its length. A profit-centred entrepreneurial economy emerged in place of subsistence farming. The introduction of coffee extended the income opportunities of independent farmer-proprietors.

Following the country's independence in 1821, the land rights of peasants were formalised on an individual basis. But while the previous communal rights were transformed into private rights, the social dimension was safeguarded by the use of fiscal tools. The primary instrument was the capture of rents for the benefit of all citizens. This was affirmed by the way in which the new highways were funded. As the World Bank reports:

> Because of coffee, land became valuable, and in an egalitarian society this early definition of individual property rights contributed to both growth and equity.[6]

The connection between land values and public investment in roads and other infrastructure was understood.

> Speculative rent resulting from such public investments was particularly significant in Guanacaste with the completion of the Pan-American Highway in the 1950s, the massive programme to build local roads in the early 1960s, the large state investments in agro-industrial production and processing in the mid-1970s, the establishment of the Guanacaste irrigation project in the late 1970s and 1980s, and

---

5 World Bank (1993: 63).
6 World Bank (1993: 64).

– most recently – the creation of a sizable network of parks and protected areas in the North of the province.[7]

The immediate beneficiaries of a new highway were the owners of land served by the road. Costa Rica introduced a Road Tax, with the rates set by municipalities. The tax was paid by anyone who benefited from access to the road. In practice, this meant that roads were funded directly out of the rents of the land in their catchment areas. In other words, the roads were self-funding. They facilitated an increase in productivity, and the net gains surfaced as an increase in land values which were used to fund the capital cost of the highway. Everyone gained and no-one lost. It was this model of infrastructure development that could have defrayed the cost of the railway. That did not happen, but this was a rare example of the failure of governance. Costa Rica redeemed herself in the way she employed taxes to fund the public's welfare.

Fiscal Freedom

COSTA RICA's philosophy of securing access to land was matched by the language of fiscal freedom. That language, however, did not go uncontested (see Box 10:1). There *were* shortcomings in the definition and application of the taxes. Nonetheless, they enshrined the spirit of enterprise and liberty.

- In 1939 the Territorial Tax was created as a charge on real estate worth more than 10,000 colones. The proceeds are divided between central government, municipalities and the Social Security Fund.
- Land not subject to the Territorial Tax is liable to a Tax on Location of Real Property. The rates are lower than for the Territorial Tax and they vary according to location. Squatters are also liable for this charge.
- The Tax on Uncultivated Land acts a disincentive to hoarding unused land. Elsewhere in Latin America, proprietors amass

---

7 Edelman (1992: 251).

Box 10:1   Coups & Growing Pains

ALFREDO GONZÁLES FLORES, who was elected as a young president (he was in his late 30s), incurred the wrath of the United Fruit Company and other rent-seekers. He had brought ideas back from the United States where, at the beginning of the 20th century, America experienced a progressive era. This was partly influenced by Henry George's book *Progress and Poverty* (1879).

George explained that the rents of land were the natural source of revenue for a modern government. In 1913, Flores ordered the modernisation of Costa Rica's fiscal system. He introduced a Bill to establish progressive taxation, to draw foreign nationals into the revenue system. He enacted a law to establish a Cadastral Survey or Land Census and Registry. This was necessary to facilitate his proposed Land Tax Bill and the Public Works of Special and Local Interest Bill. Flores wanted the beneficiaries of public works to fund the costs of infrastructure.

This mobilised the land monopolists. "The economic and political elite did not accept the attempts at reform – and decreed the fall of Gonzáles Flores."[1] The United Fruit Company and other US business interests backed the coup of 1917 which unseated Flores.

But President Woodrow Wilson refused to recognise the new government. He had staffed his cabinet with tax reformers like Louis F. Post, who favoured the tax shift on to land and away from labour. The new government in San José was deemed illegitimate. Washington enforced a Non-Recognition Policy. The country was economically isolated. The new government was short-lived, and the Flores doctrines survived to be formally adopted in law in the 1940s.

1 Salazar (1981).

---

holdings without paying for the infrastructure that gives value to their land. That is not acceptable in Costa Rica.

Five taxes are levied on the transfer of property, three of which are gift and estate taxes. The proceeds from one of them are devoted to education. Other hypothecated taxes are levied on estates. The Welfare Tax, for example, funds various welfare institutions. The University Tax supports the University of Costa Rica. The Hospital Tax is levied on the transfer of property and is split among hospitals, while the

Municipal Stamp Tax generates revenue reserved for municipalities (the tax rate must be approved by the central government).

The detail of these charges may be criticised. The Territorial Tax, for example, is levied on real estate defined as land, buildings, permanent crops and machinery. This is not the ideal revenue base. To achieve the best results, improvements on the land ought to be excluded, for taxes on them deter investment. The charge ought to be levied exclusively on the rental surplus of the land itself (treated, for fiscal purposes, as if it were in an unimproved state). And the variety of estate taxes are also unnecessarily complicated and could be consolidated into charges on the pure rent imputed to land, to reflect the services enjoyed by its occupants.

Nonetheless, the fiscal philosophy affirms the social character of land. Although one of the smallest countries in the region, "of the total of 12.6m acres of land in the country, between 6.4 and 6.6m acres are farm property – under cultivation, in pastures, and forested – giving Costa Rica the highest percentage of farmland area of all the Central American countries".[8] There was room for improvement. Marc Edelman reports that the tax on unproductive lands was not high enough to oblige owners to put all their land to use. This was illustrated in the case of a hacienda in Guanacaste. The owners sought compensation after their land was invaded by thousands of peasants. The owners of Miravalles had declared the value of their land for tax purposes at 438,115 colones ($66,131 in 1965). This assessed value dated back to 1949. Under the law, this should have been the basis for compensation. The legal battle lasted for 10 years. In the meantime, the squatters founded a small town (La Fortuna) and established farms and businesses for themselves. The occupants were willing to pay 50 colones ($7.50) per 0.7 hectare, but the owners demanded 250 colones ($37.75) per 0.7 hectare. The public agency which negotiated the expropriation could only compensate the owners at the value they had declared for tax purposes.[9]

---

8 Blutstein *et. al.*(1970: 224).
9 Edelman (1992: 267). In the event, the owners of the hacienda successfully appealed to the Costa Rican supreme court, which ruled in their favour. They received a sum greater than the assessed value of 1949: 150 colones per 0.7 hectare, a total of 2.8m colones.

Costa Rica's fiscal philosophy integrated the principles of justice into a dynamic commercial land market. This made it possible to carry over the social contract of the 19th century coffee economy into the modern era.

- In the countryside, people who want to work on land can secure grants from the state on favourable terms. This is not an inducement to amass underused property. Revenue from the tax on idle land (the rate of which varies in proportion to the amount of uncultivated land) is channelled to the Institute of Land and Settlement, which was created to facilitate the redeployment of people onto land.
- If land is expropriated by the state, compensation is paid at the value declared for tax purposes – an incentive not to under-assess the value of holdings to reduce tax liability.
- In towns, wage-workers share in the benefits of the nation's land values through free access to public amenities (health, education and welfare services) which are funded in part out of direct levies on rent.

In the democratic processes of the modern urban economy, the rise of a middle class was able to consolidate the egalitarian ethic of the countryside. The World Bank summarised the economic process leading to this outcome in these terms:

> Whereas in the past the distribution of rents and all the fruits of trade and development had been mostly governed by market forces and technology and economic circumstances, the distribution of the annually created rents of the post-1950 era took place mainly in the political arena, through both explicit and implicit taxes and subsidies.[10]

Unlike the "progressive" taxes that fund Europe's Welfare States, taxes in Costa Rica ensure that the people on the lowest incomes enjoy

---
10 World Bank (1993: 11-12).

the highest share of benefits from public expenditure. Their benefits (55% of public expenditures) were about twice as large as their taxes (27% of total tax payments), which "had a favourable redistributive impact".[11]

If we were to single out one explanation for these outcomes, it would be this statement in the World Bank report on the rural sector in the pre-modern era: "Taxation discouraged large land holdings, and possession was denied to none".[12] The result was an economy which, when the opportunity to modernise the urban sector came, would result in a rapid increase in job opportunities (at least 75% of the labour force became salaried).[13] Average wages increased faster than the legal minimum wage, an effect which could not be attributed to unionisation.[14] As the World Bank reported: "Competition for labour in the coffee regions ensured that workers would share in the increased prosperity of the country's coffee economy".[15] This exercised a benign knock-on effect on the urban wages.

To facilitate modernisation, Costa Rica adopted the complimentary policy for the industrial sector. To encourage diversification, in 1959 Congress passed a law which stimulated capital formation by exempting from income tax people who adapted to industrial forms of value-adding enterprise. They were also exempted from national and municipal taxes on invested capital.[16] Thus, fiscal policy was further shifted in favour of raising revenue from land rents while increasing the incentives for people who invested in production.

The outcome is reflected in the results reported in Table 10:1. Before 1948, Costa Rica outperformed the other countries on the isthmus in terms of *per capita* income, but thereafter the gap widened markedly. The rate of growth of income accelerated at a faster pace. This generated the rents that funded improvements to the quality of people's lives. Compared with their neighbours, the people of Costa Rica enjoyed a

---

11 World Bank (1993: 53). For an account of how low-income people subsidise the asset-values of the rich in Britain, see Harrison (2006b).
12 World Bank (1993: 128).
13 World Bank (1993: 139).
14 World Bank (1993: 139).
15 World Bank (1993: 368).
16 World Bank (1993: 86).

rise in life expectancy, a drop in child mortality and poverty rates, and almost universal literacy.

People who chose to remain in the agricultural sector also enjoyed a rise in living standards. First, output was higher on small holdings (*minifundios*) than on extensive plantations (*latifundios*) – by a significant margin. A study that compared Costa Rica with Chile, Colombia and Peru, showed that whereas *latifundios* occupied 23 times as much land as *minifundios*, the amount of cultivated land was only 6.5 times as much. And although the quality of land held by the *minifundistas* was inferior to that held by the *latifundistas*, the average value of production per hectare on *minifundios* as a multiple of that on *latifundios* is higher: for Argentina (1960), the multiple was 8, for Brazil (1960) 5, Chile (1955) 8, Colombia (1960) 14, Ecuador (1954) 3, and Guatemala (1950) 4. These findings were an acute embarrassment for the guardians of economic orthodoxy. Consequently, the differences were rationalised and justified in these terms: "*latifundio* land is farmed extensively with capital as against labour intensive production. This is reasoned to be an 'efficient' way of avoiding having to supervise peasant workers".[17]

Table 10: 1   Major Social Indicators of Central American countries

	Under-five child mortality rate (per 1,000 live births) 1995	Life expectancy at birth (years) 1994	No Access to safe water (percent) 1990-1996	No Access to health services (percent) 1990	Human Poverty Index (percent) 1994	Adult Illiteracy Rates (percent) 1995
Costa Rica	16	76.6	4	20	6.6	5.2
El Salvador	40	69.3	31	44	28.0	28.5
Guatemala	67	65.6	36	66	35.5	44.4
Honduras	38	68.4	13	34	22.0	27.3
Nicaragua	60	67.3	47	17	27.2	34.3

Source: Wilson (1998).

---

17   R Shaw (1976: 31).

Peasant workers are more efficient than the (often absentee) owners of large holdings. And yet, the preference for capital is justified in terms of efficiency – the owner (we are told) is relieved of the responsibility of keeping an eagle eye on his employees. But does he really hold land on a large scale so that he can be efficient in the use of capital, instead of labour? In reviewing studies into patterns of land ownership in South America, Paul Shaw summarises the findings in these terms:

> Most studies point out that land is owned as an inflationary hedge, as a tax write-off, or for prestige or power reasons. In all cases, accounts of large proportions of either cultivated or irrigated land lying idle are given. In Chile, for example, it was found that 50% of irrigated land on 401 farms was lying idle and in a later study found that out of 479,000 hectares, 44% of the land in natural pastures was lying idle.[18]

The apologists for current property rights smear the willingness of peasants to work (without supervision). Might the "idle" soubriquet, however, be more reasonably directed against the owners of *latifundios*?

Some critics suggest that Costa Rica's social contract was a blemished deal. We can acknowledge that this was not heaven on earth. But historians who strain to incorporate caveats into the interpretation of the Costa Rican model ought to balance their critiques with assessments of the appalling records of her neighbours.

The distribution of land was the crucial reason why Costa Rica remained stable while her neighbours engaged in civil wars. The take-off phase for Costa Rica into relative economic prosperity was supported by the willingness of a large part of its population to remain in the countryside. They worked on their land while also receiving their share of the social rents through the increase in public spending. The larger holdings of the Costa Rican peasant, compared to those in countries like Peru, Chile and Colombia, meant that he could derive a higher income from his land; an income that he could supplement by *volunteering* to work for wages outside the growing season.

---

18 Shaw (1976: 31).

Costa Rica did not have an advantage over the other countries in demographic growth terms. It had a comparatively high growth rate, which it was nevertheless better able to support than were her neighbours. Costs Rica's small farms were double the size of those in other countries. Thus, there was less inducement to seek employment in the cities, where displaced people tend to congregate in the slums to eke out an existence in the informal economy or by resorting to crime.

Academics who acknowledge the need to factor land into their analyses of poverty and under-development in developing countries continue to play with a superficial and contrived model of land markets. Even critics of the land privatisation doctrine fail to recognise the significance of tax policies as inextricably bound up with the way the land market operates. Annelies Zoomers, an associate professor in human geography at the Center for Latin American Research and Documentation in Amsterdam, in research that is otherwise admirable in chronicling the neo-liberal model of land rights favoured by the West, claims:

> In the first place, despite all the adjustments, land policy is still based on the same set of old key principles (i.e., the need to promote markets to facilitate efficiency-enhancing transfers to the better and more efficient producers). Faith in land markets and the healthy operation of the price mechanism remain the central ideas… Given the multi-functionality of land, the price mechanism cannot be expected to lead to an allocation that is optimal in all respects.[19]

But while stating the need to address issues beyond those of farm sizes and legal status, Zoomers fails to take into account the impact of the fiscal environment. If she had done so, the role of markets and prices would be seen in a different light. Taxes are the public's pricing mechanism. When that mechanism is incorrectly structured, distortions arise to impede a fluid allocation and use of land to deliver optimum results both for the individual and for society.

---

19 Zoomers and Haar (2000: 293).

To assess statistics on land holding, in isolation, is dangerous. They tend to distract social scientists, who in the Costa Rican case are drawn by the raw numbers to conclude that "despite the state's efforts at agrarian reform and Costa Rica's image as a land of yeomen, the land-holding pattern remains remarkable unequal".[20] This ignores the evidence of how the benefits from the nation's land are shared. A comprehensive audit would take into account the way in which rent is taxed and shared among everyone through public sector services, including peasants on their minifundios. The rent-funded "social wage" received by small farmers (through, for example, access to health and education services) raises the standard of living well above the condition of the *minifundistas* in the other Latin countries.

Costa Rica's political process is sufficiently robust to enable coalitions of communists and libertarians to cooperate in the national interest. One result has been a high level of investment in infrastructure regardless of the political colour of the administration in power,[21] the benefits of which are shared according to the norms of justice.

---

20 Edelman and Kenen, *The Costs Rica Reader*, p. 126.
21 Jakobstein (1987: 225).

Chapter 11
Truth and Reconciliation

THE truth about organised violence requires an honest account of the colonial influence, but reconciliation requires sovereign nations to take responsibility for their affairs. Sufficient time has passed, to enable former colonies to re-align their constitutions according to the principles of justice. That they have failed to do so is demonstrated by the serious political stresses that threaten the 21st century prosperity of India because its leaders have failed to address the flaws inherited from a 19th century colonial master.

In 1967, a group of insurgents called Naxalites threatened civil order in West Bengal. The Maoist-led rebellion was driven by grievances over access to land. Today, as India chases China in the league of big-time growth rates, Naxalites are disrupting the world's largest democracy with violent tactics. The rebels have built strongholds throughout the rural sub-continent. They succeeded in West Bengal, largely because of a locally applied land reform. But, as the *Financial Times* editorialised on February 15, 2010:

> Today, the need is to provide education and health, land and jobs to offer hope and opportunity. This is not just about restoring law and order to ungoverned areas. It is about giving tens of millions of outcast Indians their first stake in modern India.

The Naxalites are now making in-roads into urban areas. Their grudge is no longer against the British who distorted patterns of land ownership in Bengal two centuries ago; their complaint is with successive socialist governments which failed to define a constitutional settlement that included everyone in the post-colonial prosperity that was possible under conditions of freedom. But, even today, India's major political parties are unable to specify *why* their policies are incapable of emancipating all their citizens. Has the time come for it to create a truth and reconciliation commission (TRC)?

Over past 20 years, governments have used commissions to try and establish the truth about the civil conflicts that ruptured their countries. The aim was to reconcile combatants and rebuild their communities. From Latin America through Africa and to Indonesia in Asia, the TRCs excavated evidence about violent deeds that might otherwise have remained buried, poisoning people's relationships, as the victims - denied justice - nursed untreated wounds.

The TRCs produced millions of words in evidence and recommendations, but did they identify root causes? Societies which needed to uncover and deal with the full truth included Argentina, Chile, Sierra Leone, Rwanda and the most famous of them all – South Africa, whose commission was chaired by Desmond Tutu, the Anglican archbishop whose opposition to apartheid earned him the Nobel Prize for Peace.

Nations need to interrogate the nature of systemic violence if they wish to come to terms with their past so that they may (like Canada and Australia) make amends for colonial misdeeds (but see Box 11:1).

The goal is the rehabilitation of social space. The challenge is to confront the past events that undermine current perceptions. The task is a painful one. The US, for example, teaches its young that America originated as a champion of people's freedom. Would it subject itself to a Truth Commission? Most people in the US acknowledge the gap between the promise of "the Democracy" and the treatment of tribal peoples and other minorities. There were repeated investigations into episodes such as the 1864 Sand Creek Massacre, in which the inhabitants of a Cheyenne village were slaughtered. But such investigations were

> ### Box 11:1 Australia's Apology
>
> LIKE Canada, Australia attempted to solve its aboriginal problem by kidnapping children and raising them in ways that would strain out the genetic codes that differentiated them from the offspring of the colonial settlers. In 2008, Prime Minister Kevin Rudd publicly apologised for that disgraceful exercise, and agreed to devote resources to help the first settlers. But because of the prevailing laws, and disrespect for other people's ecological traditions, a settlement based on justice appeared to be beyond reach. Kate Grenville explained:
>
>> When a culture has been as thoroughly disrupted as indigenous culture has been by European colonisation over the last 200 years, the damage can't be easily reversed. That culture, and the hunter-gatherer life it sprang from, can't be put back the way it was. At the same time, it can't be erased: "assimilation" isn't the way to go.[1]
>
> Grenville, an award-winning author, observed that, despite the additional government money, housing – and traditions related to the occupation of land – continued to bedevil the terms on which to equalise the life chances of the aboriginal population.
>
> 1 Grenville (2010).

carried out not in a dialectic of contrition and confession, but with the full-throated self-confidence of an expanding, militarily triumphant state then consolidating an exceptional sense of national purpose. Even as it waged an eliminationist war against Native Americans, for instance, the US government could claim that its investigation into the 'brutal and cowardly acts' that took place in Sand Creek was 'vindicating the cause of justice and upholding the honor of the nation.'[1]

The intention was to enable nations to step beyond reconciliation. But without a thorough examination of the impact of systems of positive law conveying privileges and property rights, and the associated distribution of income, it is not possible to draw general conclusions about the violent features of certain aspects of ownership rights in land. Without that general context, pathological forms of behaviour and institutions such as apartheid are relegated to the past as if their influences have been nullified. That, of course, relieves politicians of

---

1 Grandin and Klubock (2007: 100)

the responsibility to identify the reforms that would liberate everyone.

Previous commission reports have been criticised for distracting people from the whole truth. Critics claimed that the commissions were biased – perhaps with the exception of Guatemala's – by too narrow a mandate. They focused on the individual – the pain of victims, the evil deeds of perpetrators – while sidelining the historical and institutional contexts within which the conflicts were conducted. A simple narrative was favoured, in which two factions raised arms and were hell-bent on destroying each other, with the general population suffering as the collateral damage. This critique is well founded, but could – should – it have been otherwise? Understanding the social roots of violence is imperative, but when is it appropriate to conduct the radical inquest?

Countless numbers died in the wars of liberation that seemingly brought colonialism to an end, and in the civil wars that followed independence competing indigenous leaders vied with one another for political control. Here and there, but certainly not universally, populations attempted to adjust their laws to include the millions who had previously been excluded from society. The TRCs were established to prevent further blood letting, driven by the desire for revenge of the victors; and to rebuild war-torn societies. So, in the circumstances, it may be understandable that care was taken to limit the mandate for establishing the historical truth. The immediate aftermath of violent conflict may not be the best time to form a mature judgment on the complexities associated with the killing of a million people, as happened in Mozambique. Whose truth about the conflict could be objective and factual? The combatants would have submitted to the TRCs their opposed visions of the circumstances that provoked the violence, visions that necessarily inspired their expectations about the future. Against them would be the incumbent power, which would insist that they were defending law and order.

In the former colonial territories, opposition forces, in almost all cases, were animated by the language of Marxism. The Marxist paradigm prevailed because its violent rhetoric – as a tool of class conflict – expressed the needs of dispossessed peoples. Peasants had to be mobilised against armies equipped with sophisticated weaponry manufactured in Europe, the USA and the USSR, so they needed a doctrine that legitimised violence and motivated poorly-equipped people pursuing their rights.

How could a panel of truth-seekers make sense of such conflicting world views? Might the truth have prolonged the use of violence? Might the ideological contest, have led to flawed conclusions? And might that have lead to flawed remedies?

In setting the TRCs in a benign light, we cannot deny that they were used to skew the knowledge that was made available to the general population. The manipulation of minds was the result of the self-interest of external agencies intent on promoting their visions of the future. An example is provided by the cynical exploitation of the Guatemalan TRC by the US Agency for International Development (USAID: see Box 11:2)

A society whose "truth and reconciliation" exercise fails to identify the whole truth must be treated with understanding. Wounds need

Box 11:2   What Price Democracy?

GUATEMALA'S Commission for Historical Clarification explored issues beyond the misdeeds of individuals. It censured acts of genocide against the Mayan people in the 1980s. The conflict, lasting 34 years, claimed the lives of about 200,000 people. Over 90% of the human rights violations, according to the commission, could be laid at the doors of agencies of the state.

The report offered "illustrative cases of massacres in the highlands [which] showed the history of land struggles these communities faced, and how they were organized".[1] The findings were widely disseminated by USAID, allegedly to help the healing process. A TV serial was funded with millions of dollars, along with educational materials, so that the masses would be aware of the evidence.

But the televised treatments contained very little historical content – explaining the cultural context of the violence – and Washington censured references to the role of the US in sponsoring the CIA's overthrow of the democratically elected president, Jacobo Arbenz, in 1954. The CIA's intervention, according to the commission, was a watershed event for the ensuing political violence.

[1] Oglesby (2007: 92).

time to heal, and the truth – the whole truth, and nothing but the truth – can be the biggest victim if it is sought in the heat of the moment. Nevertheless, the time must come when the quest for that truth needs to be initiated. For without it, the prospect of governments building new foundations in the post-conflict period will not be high. A tragic case study from Africa bears witness to this judgment.

The South African model of land justice

THE consignment of apartheid into history was supposed to launch South Africa on a new phase of social development. Injustices were to be eliminated through democracy.

At the heart of the legacy of the past were the injustices associated with "the land problem". In South Africa, this was to be resolved by restoring land to those who could show an ancestral claim to tracts owned by white citizens. The South African development model – driven by the political objective to restore land rights to the majority indigenous population - will ultimately fail, because of the failure to take into account all the complex economic relationships attached to systems of property rights and the associated policies that constitute the public's finance.

Restoring land to claimants now has a record of evidence accumulated over 12 years, on which to assess the fairness – and efficiency – of this route to justice. On a research trip to South Africa I was able to examine the ANC government's approach at close quarters. Its goal was the transfer of 30% of the arable land to black farmers by 2014.

- In the decade up to 2008, just 4% of the land has been transferred. Government officials privately conceded that they will not achieve their target by 2014.
- The government promised to accelerate the transfer of about 5m hectares to black farmers – equal to the whole of the amount of land transferred in the previous 12 years. Logistically (admitted officials) this will not be possible.
- To accelerate the transfer of land, an Expropriation Bill (to override resistance from white farmers) was prepared. The government then abandoned the Bill.

Compounding the political problem is the unfolding threat to the food security of South Africa. White farmers whose properties have been "Gazetted" (notice served that their land was under claim) are legally prohibited from investing in their farms. I visited two examples in the Limpopo region: fields have remained fallow for years because the owners were legally restrained from increasing production by investing in their orchards. Properties transferred from white commercial farmers, meanwhile, are routinely abandoned by their new owners, the capital investments vandalised and sold for trivial sums, the fields no longer growing food. Orange trees on citrus farms are dying from neglect; and being chopped down for firewood. Much of this was, in part, the outcome of the de-skilling of black farm workers during the period of apartheid.

I examined in detail a tea plantation which once employed 6,000 people in peak season. The hillsides are weed-choked, the processing and packing plant has been demolished (it looks like a bomb hit it), the working equipment sold off. A hillside of brick-built dwellings which housed families of the plantation's employees is now occupied by ghosts.

In 2008, for the first time, South Africa became a net importer of food. The Limpopo region's politicians say that, soon, they will be buying "South African food" from Mozambique – meaning, having to import food produced by white South African farmers who have relocated in Mozambique. South Africa's balance of payments will be negatively affected; but the social costs for communities throughout the productive regions of South Africa cannot be calculated.

In South Africa, we are witnessing the unfolding – in slow motion – of the process that brought Zimbabwe to its knees: the inability of its leaders to define a land policy that unites the population behind peace and prosperity for everyone.

Community Land Trusts

CAN a fiscal approach address the problems visible on the ground in South Africa?

Many white farmers claim to want to resolve the land issue to the satisfaction of claimants (they acknowledge the historical injustices), but their warning of an implosion of food production is dismissed as self-serving by ANC politicians. There is no constructive dialogue of the kind that could lead to a new policy orientation. The government is determined to push forward with land restoration for those who can demonstrate a historical association with tracts of land. With the best will in the world, one cannot be optimistic about the outcome.

But there is a practical way to simultaneously resolve the need to

- maintain the output of food, and increase employment, in the rural sector;
- address the grievances of people whose ancestors were dispossessed; and
- retain the expertise of white farmers, to stem the exodus to Australia and South America.

According to South Africa's constitution, the land belongs to all citizens. Thus, to redistribute part of the land to a minority of black citizens does not respect the terms of the constitution. In fact, by privileging a minority – but only a minority - of black citizens, the spatial discrimination that defined apartheid is carried over to the democratic era. This is not what the ANC intended; but it is the reality *on the ground*.

Equity, in all its senses, is served when we shift from thinking about land as a physical entity, to land as the source of a flow of income; an income that flows into the public purse. This financial model as a problem-solver would have several benefits for agriculture.

White farmers want to remain on the land to produce commercial crops. They love the land every bit as much as the people who were originally dispossessed, so there is little to gain from exploring who has the deepest affinity with the land. White farmers, in their philosophical reflections, say that, of course, *nobody* can really own the land, because such a notion is fatuous. *Land is God-given*, they volunteer, and we are no more than stewards on it.

Policy: white farmers should be helped to see the wisdom of accepting that, while they may retain the title deeds to the land, the *whole* of the economic rent of land must be treated as the public's revenue. In return, taxes on their labour, and on the undepreciated value of investment on the land, would be commensurately reduced.

Black claimants must be helped to understand that *all black citizens* of South Africa were dispossessed by white settlers, and by the resettlement laws promulgated in the 20th century. Therefore, a formula is needed that restores land justice to *all* black citizens, not just the relatively few who can prove a historical connection with particular tracts.

Policy: black claimants should accept that (at present) they do not possess the skills and capital to work commercial farms.[2] If they want to become farmers, they have an obligation to prepare themselves so that they can put the land to its best use not just for themselves, but for the rest of the population that needs food. The ANC government can best unite the nation behind the ethic of sharing *not the land* but the rent of the land of South Africa, in a way that synchronises – in a visible way – the mutual interests of all ethnic groups.

An example of this policy focus would be the re-skilling of people who want to work as farmers. Retaining people in the countryside is imperative. How might this be done? The following is partly based on suggestions from white farmers who recognise the urgent need to raise the skills base among the black population.

Why not create, in each region, a Community Land Trust? The Trust could assume responsibility for *facilitating* certain activities that engaged *all* citizens – as equals – in the progressive resolution of current problems. One example: funding a network of "land grant" agricultural colleges.[3] These would provide a 3-year training in the skills of farming. They could also serve as facilitators of satellite

---

2 About 90% of land claimants have no experience of working agricultural land, according to a senior official of the Agricultural and Lands Department in the Limpopo region (interview, June 2008). Furthermore (he said), the new "farmers" acquire the land with no working capital, an extreme reluctance to borrow money from banks, and no marketing expertise. In the main, the government has been unable to provide the financial support to enable the claimants to establish viable farming enterprises.

3 In 19th century America, colleges were established throughout the US with grants of land on which to establish their activities. The politicians who conceived this plan wanted to advance America's capacity for research and development. Land grant colleges, which became universities, helped to lay the foundations of the commercial success of the US in the 20th century, by giving it a competitive advantage in R&D.

farming operations: nurturing small-scale, intensive food-producing units owned and administrated by college graduates. The college could provide marketing support (operating like a co-operative for graduate farmers). As the students acquired their diplomas and developed a track record for earning income from growing food, so they would become credit-worthy. Those who wished to do so would be able to borrow money to acquire the hectares that turned them into full-scale commercial entrepreneurs.

The finance for the agricultural colleges would come from the Community Land Trust, which would be funded out of the land rents of their region.

- White farmers would continue to work "their" land, while paying rent into the public purse and ensuring the country remained one of Africa's "bread-baskets".
- Black citizens with aspirations to own land would know that their children, in the meantime, were being educated to become skilled farmers out of "their" land-rents.
- Citizens who do not want to farm the land would nonetheless enjoy a share of "their" land rents – for the rents of South Africa are sufficient to fund the education, health and welfare of all children.

This political and philosophical paradigm would rebuild South Africa on a multi-cultural basis. The alternative is the current policy, which is failing at the inter-communal level. In 2008, South Africans in shanty towns murdered about 50 people in street violence. The victims were refugees from Zimbabwe, who fled Mugabe and the governance that failed to resolve that country's land problem.

The most troubling of all, however, is that South Africa is nurturing a new generation of children whose attitudes are grounded in distrust and violence.[4] We will now address the question of whether

---

4 Data has been compiled by the Agency for Social Reconstruction, a developmental consultancy in Johannesburg.

it is possible to develop a programme of non-violent governance for complex societies in the globalised world of the 21st century.

CHAPTER 12

PRINCIPLES OF NON-VIOLENT GOVERNANCE

SOCIAL scientists seek to explain violent deeds in a variety of ways, but almost always locating the behaviour in terms of the character of the individual. The vulgarised version of the theory of evolution – summarised as the "survival of the fittest" – is one of the slickest paraphrases of what they want a scientific theory to mean. And yet, Charles Darwin, in *The Descent of Man*, stressed the sociability of humans. Anarchist Peter Kropotkin, who emphasised mutual aid as a driver of evolution, observed that "Darwin was quite right when he saw in man's social qualities the chief factor for his evolution, and Darwin's vulgarisers are entirely wrong when they maintain the contrary".[1]

The debate around the theory of evolution, and how it shaped the destiny of *homo sapiens*, remains controversial,[2] and will have to be revisited. First, however, we need to dispel the inanities that reinforce the belief that violence cannot be eliminated because it is "natural".

When a lion brings down a gazelle, to feed her cub, the violence derives its meaning from the biological context inscribed by nature. What meaning do we ascribe to the torture of prisoners by US military personnel in Baghdad's Abu Ghraib prison? To the deaths of millions in the trenches of World War I? To the genocidal destruction of the Mayans by the Spaniards? These were not the acts of psychological deviants. If we deprive acts of violence of their historical and cultural

---

1 Kropotkin (1987).
2 Pichot (2009).

contexts, we deprive them of their meaning. But properly viewed, they testify to the impoverishment of the spiritual, ethical and social content of the beings concerned.

The term "banality of evil" was coined by Hannah Arendt (1906-1975) in her account of the Nazi Holocaust. Such deeds, she argued, were perpetrated by ordinary people who accepted the directives of their state. So they participated in genocide on the basis that their actions were normal. But attributing horrendous acts to the personal failings of individuals suits those who benefit from the privileges created by capitalism as it is at present constituted.

Convictions against individuals for "crimes against humanity" serve a cathartic purpose. Legal rituals offered by criminal tribunals in The Hague exonerate – distract attention from – the historical and cultural framework that incubated the crimes. Cleansed of those individual acts of evil, which could not be ignored, the socially violent system is free to continue to deprive people of their rights.

The perpetrators of genocide must be held to personal account, because each of us has a moral duty to resist orders that are contrary to natural justice and our humanity. But we also need to pronounce verdicts on social systems that fail abjectly to secure peace and prosperity for everyone, as occurred in the 1930s. For it was that failure which created the fertile ground that could be seeded by fanatics like Adolf Hitler. There have been no show trials against the social system that incubated Hitler. One consequence is the economic instability of the first decade of the 21st century, which is once again recruiting people to fascism. Politicians like Frenchman Jean-Marie Le Pen exploit the anxieties associated with the loss of jobs and homes. Le Pen, for example, used the European Parliament, of which he was an elected member, to insist that the Nazi gas chambers and the Holocaust were mere details of history.[3]

Language, as well as our institutions, need to be reformed. Acts of brutality that are described as "mindless", for example, lead us to believe that perpetrators are in some way out of control. If that were the reality, there can be little hope for the future. But I have attempted

---

3   Traynor (2009).

to show that, when dealing with violence on its organised scale, a "mind" – representing a logic – is very much behind the events that have disgraced modern history. Hitler was the product of a corrupt social system. That does not relieve him of his personal responsibilities. But the cause of humanity is not served by ignoring the social conditions that made it possible for a nation to assign him the power to behave in the way that he did.

For the benefit of inspired leaders like Barack Obama, we need to reframe the debate over what constitutes a benevolent form of society and its matching market economy. We need to renew the values and processes that made our species possible. But rehabilitation has to be funded: we need to recover the community's surplus product, the material resources that finance cultural innovation and sustain it through evolutionary time-scales. A case that needs to be closely studied is the first modern nation to voluntarily agree to de-militarize itself.

Everyday Seeds of Violence

COSTA RICA's success, like Botswana's in southern Africa,[4] is based on the idea that natural assets are social in character, and therefore ought to fund social development. But the transformation of these two countries is based on an incomplete political philosophy, which is why their model of governance does need further development. We may judge this claim in relation to the crisis of 1980, which put at risk the Costa Rican model.

Costa Rica came close to integrating the principles of justice with land tenure. To further evolve that model, however, she needed to remain independent of the Western philosophical virus that seeks to standardise the capitalist model throughout the world. She almost lost that independence when she led herself into the jaws of the International Monetary Fund (IMF).

Hitherto, the vitality embedded in Costa Rica's social foundations inoculated her against the poison in the chalice known as the Washington Consensus.

---

4 Harrison (2008).

Costa Rica was a pioneer among Latin American countries, in the sense that it was the first to show concern for the social cost of adjustment. Thus, it was able to implement far-reaching adjustment and stabilisation measures without provoking the popular backlashes in other countries, such as Argentina, Brazil, the Dominican Republic and Venezuela.[5]

So what drove Costa Rica to risk its social contract by accepting the IMF's "adjustment and stabilisation measures" in the 1980s?

A financial crisis struck which Costa Rica could not resolve on her own. The IMF intervened and recovery of the economy began in 1983 under the supervision of its ideologues. The outcome was a shock to the population, and the onset of trends with which we are now familiar in other developing countries.

> In terms of macro-economic policy, the former practice of a gradual application of adjustment policies ended, resulting in a deterioration of fiscal and external equilibria and the implementation of drastic 'shock' stabilisation measures. This in turn led to a slowing down of growth and an increase in poverty.[6]

Costa Rica could blame no-one but herself. Government policies permitted a speculation-driven real estate cycle. The country was allowed to drift into a classic land-led boom/bust property crisis. The drama unfolded over 18 years.

- On the back of its successful social policies, Cost Rica's productivity rose dramatically between 1960 and 1980. Urbanisation increased, driving up the demand for housing and commercial space. This was reflected in the rise in land values.
- GDP *per capita* nearly doubled. The country acquired the means to fund job-creating capital formation. But because a

---

5 Garnier *et al* (1997: 369).
6 Garnier *et al* (1997: 371).

part of the rents generated by the economy remained in the private domain, an increasing proportion of national income was diverted into land speculation.

The ensuing dislocation was mis-represented as a "financial crisis", rather than a failure of governance. The diagnosis was incorrect, as was the response – seeking salvation in the arms of the IMF.

The crisis was inevitable, once government failed to reserve the rent of urban land to fund the public services that raised the productivity of the economy. Speculators gambled on future windfalls. This created a boom in asset prices that fuelled the further growth in credit in a self-fulfilling vicious circle of monetary expansion, from which there was one outcome only: a price "correction". Recession followed.

Policy errors infected the countryside. Government wanted to encourage the livestock sector. It enabled cattle ranchers to borrow money at low or negative rates of interest. This, in itself, was *not* the problem. But given the structure of taxation, economists advising the politicians should have explained that there would consequently be a rapid rise in rural land prices. Owners of the best land would capitalise the cheap credit into higher prices.

Errors were further compounded by the way government funded new highways and electrification, which would increase productivity and raise land values. Theory[7] tells us that the rise in the rents that people are willing to pay for access to newly serviced locations were *not* the problem. If those rents had been used to pay for the capital invested in the infrastructure, growth would not have been interrupted. But by allowing publicly-created rents to be privatised, government sponsored the speculation that distorted patterns of consumption, investment and saving. Boom. And then, bust.

The theory was confirmed by facts on the ground. Entrepreneurs who established their dairy activities during the early phase of rural development, bought land at cheap rates, before the investment in infrastructure. In Rio Frío, farmers "captured greater benefits through land appreciation given the initial level of infrastructure". The increase

---

7 Gaffney (2010).

in land value was 84%, "reflecting investments of public funds not recaptured by the government through tax appreciation".[8]

The reduced costs of transporting milk to market along the paved roads, and the gains from access to electricity, yielded financial benefits that could be estimated in advance. The income transfer to owners who purchased land before 1980 in Rio Frío was $36,887. In Sonafluca, the fortunate ones pocketed $41,887.[9] That money could have been reinvested in public services for the benefit of everyone. That, in turn, would have avoided the public sector debt which turned into a financial crisis.

By its funding policies, Costa Rica trapped itself in debts that exposed it to the doctrines of the IMF, whose Washington Consensus betrayed the ideals of a country that was consciously building a non-violent society.

Costa Rica was not alone in delivering itself to the mercies of a perverse economic doctrine. But why couldn't that country's economic advisers detect the pitfalls of allowing rents to be privatised? Economics suffers from an amnesia that enables its practitioners to ignore the process described above. Even economists who reflect on the dividend from peace fail to recognise that the land market undermines the quest to eliminate conflict. This failure features in a study commissioned by Australia's Institute for Economics & Peace. With the onset of peace, "agriculture will benefit from the dynamic peace dividend: as economies grow on account of peace, it becomes safe again to invest in land".[10]

The *users* of land *should* pay rents for the benefit of using land, including investment in the peace-making activities delivered by the community. The anomaly arises when those rents are capitalised into selling prices and privatised. The onset of "peace" immediately re-seeds violence into society, beginning a new cycle of activities that move inexorably in the direction of conflict. The economic activities that led to the global catastrophe of 2008, for example, was in part the product of "peace" initiatives. These included the dismantling of

---

8 Holman *et al* (1992).
9 Holman *et al* (1992: Part 2, Table 13).
10 Institute for Economics & Peace (2009: 37).

the Berlin Wall in 1989. Every country in the world (following the eclipse of Soviet communism and Maoist Marxism) integrated itself into a single property cycle, culminating in a land-led boom/bust of epic proportions at the beginning of the 21st century. One index of the violence built into that business cycle was expressed by UNICEF, the UN's children's agency. It forecast the deaths of an additional 200,000-400,000 infants every year as a result of the global economic collapse.

Render Unto Caesar

HE KNEW it was a trap, so when the *agents provocateurs* questioned Jesus about his views on taxation, the reply was enigmatic.

> "Render unto Caesar the things which are Caesar's, and unto God the things that are God's" (Matthew 22:21).

He disclosed precisely nothing, but the answer served its purpose: buying Jesus more time for his mission. We, on the other hand, cannot duck the question. We need to offer a principled answer to the question of who is entitled to what in the share-out of the nation's income.

The principle on which each of us should pay the community's agencies for their services should be defined with clarity. The terms on which we formulate our individual – and social – rights and obligations, should be inscribed in a new social contract. For the future of our civilisation depends on our ability to *re-colonise our home territories*. This should not entail the violence of taking land from people who now hold it. It does mean renegotiating the terms of tenure, however, so that everyone is treated equally; and that includes everyone being allocated a stake in land.

In poverty-stricken Sub-Saharan Africa, for example, the solution to the legacy of injustice does *not* lie in the removal of white settlers from the land. Emptying the shanty towns – by repopulating the countryside or incorporating people into the formal urban economy – can be achieved by redesigning the process of development.

Scientific, spiritual, cultural and intellectual perspectives all prescribe the same solution: reform the public's pricing mechanism.

The principle that guides reform is one that people do not regard as controversial: *pay for the benefits that one receives.* This entails the funding of public services out of the rent of land and the rents of nature's resources. The policy achieves two results.

- *Redemption of the land for the benefit of everyone.*

If the landless do not acquire tracts, they *do* share in the *value of land.* Free education…clinics for the villages…social security that removes anxiety…the common space funded and shared without fear or favour. I may "own" a thousand acres; but I pay *you* your share of the rents of that land, through the exchequer, by funding the services that you and your family use in common with everyone else.

- *Stability in the production of food and exportable commodities.*

From the terrible lessons learnt from countries like Zimbabwe, we know that Africa cannot afford to lose experienced farmers. The terms on which farmers hold land can be renegotiated, *without disputes over whose name appears on title deeds.* All that is required is the democratisation of fiscal policy. *Pay the land rent to the community, and government can abolish the income and consumption taxes that reduce the living standards of farmers and their employees.* This would expand employment opportunities and raise the real value of wages.

This fiscal reform is based on an organising principle that delivers an organic balance between individuals, between the individual and society, and between nations. It reasserts the importance of cooperation in the economy. Peter Kropotkin emphasised that the elimination of competition served the evolutionary needs of humans. Mutual support within the early communities was of paramount significance in securing the conditions that enabled humans to evolve through kinship and tribal structures. In reviewing the anthropological literature, Kropotkin recognised that the key was "a union between families considered as of common descent and owning a certain territory in common".[11] But competition was also a vital aspect of the evolutionary process. Competition and co-operation are mutually compatible in a holistic community. It was the legal changes to tenure that inflicted the distortions that damaged the relationship between people and their environment, and between themselves, that then generated pathological forms of behaviour which is uncritically attributed to competition. A pricing mechanism that integrates public and private prices lays the foundation for re-creating symbiosis in the complex society.

Philosophers of the 18th and 19th centuries glimpsed this reality, and offered tentative outlines of the vision. Today, because the social sciences have been perverted to accommodate the doctrine of land privatisation, scholars are obliged to seek explanations for violence through explorations that fail to deliver answers. Kathleen Taylor, for example, adopts the approach based on neural science. Her words only permit us to infer a contest for land, with violence "contained in cultural ghettos – 'troublespots' like Israel/Palestine and Somalia or, more locally, 'problem neighbourhoods'".[12] By failing to make explicit the spatial dimension, Taylor cannot sensibly answer her question: "If the Nazis had wiped out every Jew in Europe, would Hitler's problems have come to an immediate end?"[13] By stressing the neural approach to violence, Taylor had to conclude that "the problems would remain and new scapegoats would have to be found". Of course they would, but not because of the anatomical constitution of humans: rather, because the philosophical and legal contest over living space remained unresolved.

If we fail to recognise the flaws in the foundations of society, we are led to Frankenstein-type solutions.

> A neuro-scientific approach to cruelty…leaves open another possibility: that in some not-too-distant future we may be able to modify brains directly…There is no reason why precision removal of strong and dangerous beliefs in humans should not soon be a realistic treatment. Just imagine being

---

11 Kropotkin (1987: 107-108).
12 Taylor (2009: 240).
13 Taylor (2009: 242).

able to cure the bigots in Israel and Palestine, damp down the Islamists and the racists, convert the homophobes and sexists to reasonable folk – all with a pill or a spray or some quick fix, instead of the wearisome slog of changing beliefs and reordering incentives.[14]

Most "bigots" are people whose rationality and morality are suspended because, ultimately, they are locked into contests over land. No amount of brain surgery will solve that problem. But social surgery can secure the justice that removes the need to resort to violence.

We have now learnt that there can be little change of substance while the Predators continue to defend their real estate with the contracts that cause death. Whether one approaches the principles of governance from the point of view of theology or science, the same conclusions are prescribed: the State's function is to mediate between citizens, to facilitate the need for people to meet their personal obligations. First and foremost, that entails mundane changes to the tax code. We need to restore the principle that is missing from the public's pricing mechanism: the requirement that people should pay for the benefits they derive from their participation in the community.

This principle cuts across the ideological divides, and unites people behind a common plan to renew their communities. We may summarise the proposal in these terms: *we need to re-socialise the publicly-created value, and re-privatise the personally-created value.*

With the adoption of that one principle, contests over who owns the land disappear; and with them, systemic violence.

---

14 Taylor (2009: 246).

BIBLIOGRAPHY

Ahmida, Ali Abdullatif (1994), *The Making of Modern Libya: State formation, Colonisation, and Resistance, 1830-1932*, Albany, NY: State University of New York Press.

Allen, Nick (2009), "Squatters' right to lists of homes lying empty", *Daily Telegraph*, March 21.

Ameringer, Charles D. (1982), Charles D. Ameringer, *Democracy in Costa Rica*, New York: Praeger.

Andelson, R.V. (1979), *Critics of Henry George*, Cranbury, NJ: Associated University Press.

Andelson, Robert V. (2000), *Land Value Taxation Around the World*, Third edn., Oxford: Blackwell.

Appa, Gautam and Girish Patel (1996), "Unrecognised, Unnecessary and Unjust displacement: case studies from Gujarat, India", in McDowell (1996).

Arendt, Hannah (1963), *Eichmann in Jerusalem: A Report on the Banality of Evil*, New York: Viking (revised 1968).

August, Mark (1983), "Guyana in the mood for change", *The Guardian*, October 28.

Balfour, Sebastian (2002), *Deadly Embrace: Morocco and the Road to the Spanish Civil War*, Oxford, Oxford University Press.

Balfour, Sebastian (1997), *The End of the Spanish Empire 1898-1923*, Oxford: Oxford University Press.

Bidwell, Robin (1973), *Morocco Under Colonial Rule: French Administration of Tribal Areas 1912-1956*, London: Frank Cass.

Bird, Leonard (1984), *Costa Rica: The Unarmed Democracy*, London: Sheppard Press.

Blutstein, Howard I., et. al. (1970), *Area Handbook for Costa Rica*, Washington DC: The American University.

Bodley, John H. (1982), *Victims of Progress*, Palo Alto, CA: Mayfield.

Bourguignon, Francois and Christian Morrison (2002), "Inequality among World Citizens: 1820-1992)", *The American Economic Review* 92, No. 4.

Brendon, Piers (2007), *The Decline and Fall of the British Empire 1781-1997*, London: Jonathan Cape.

Cernea, Michael M. (1996), "Understanding and preventing impoverishment from displacement: reflections on the state of knowledge", in McDowell (1996).

Chang, Ha-Joon (2008), *Bad Samaritans: the Guilty Secrets of Rich Nations & the Threat to Global Prosperity*, London: Random House.

Collier,Paul (2007), "Conflicts", in Lomborg (2007).

Coulton, G.G. (1925), *The Medieval Village*, Cambridge: University Press.

Crane, N, and M. Crane (2005), "Terrorised economies", unpublished manuscript, page 33, cited in Linotte (2007).

Day, David (2008), *Conquest: How Societies Overwhelm Others*, Oxford: Oxford University Press

Diamond, A.S. (1971), *Primitive Law Past and Present*, London: Methuen.

Diamond, Jared (2005), *Collapse: How Societies Choose to Fail or Survive*, London: Allen Lane.

Duncan, Tyrrell, Keith Jefferis and Patrick Molutsi (1997), "Botswana: social development in a resource-rich economy", in Mehrotra and Jolly (1997).

Economist Intelligence Unit (2009), *Manning the Barricades: Who's at risk as deepening economic distress foments social unrest*, London.

Edelman, Marc, and Joanne Kenen (1989), *The Costa Rica Reader*, New York: Grove Weidenfeld.

Edelman, Marc (1992), *The Logic of the Latifundio: The Large Estates of Northwestern Costa Rica Since the Late 19th Century*, Stanford: Stanford University Press.

Ekin, Des (2006), *The Stolen Village*, Dublin: O'Brien Press.

Evans, Michael and Catherine Philp (2008), "Case for military action in Zimbabwe", *The Times*, June 24.

Evans-Pritchard, E.E. (1949), *The Sanusi of Cyrenaica*, Oxford, Clarendon Press.

Foucault, Michel (2003), *Society Must be Defended* (translator: David Macey), London: Allen Lane.

Freeman, Edward A. (1869), *Old English History for Children*, London.

Gaffney, Mason (2009), *After the Crash: Designing a Depression-Free Economy*, Oxford: Wiley-Blackwell.

Garnier, Leonardo, Rebeca Grynspan, Roberto Hidalgo, Guillermo Monge and Juan Diego Trejos (1997), "Costa Rica: Social Development and Heterodox Adjustment", in Mehrotra and jolly 1997.

Geldof, Bob   (2009), "An African stimulus to help reboot the world economy", *Financial Times*, April 2.

George, Katherine   (1958), "The Civilized West Looks at Primitive Africa: 1400-1800: A study in Ethnocentrism", *Isis*, Vol. 49, No. 155, Part 1, March.

Goldberg, Jonah   (2007), *Liberal Fascism*, London: Penguin.

Govan, Fiona   (2006), "Town that breeds suicide bombers", *Daily Telegraph*, November 25.

Grandin, Greg, and Thomas Miller Klubock   (2007), "Introduction: a US Truth Commission", in Grandin and Klubock (2007).

Grandin, Greg, and Thomas Miller Klubock (eds.)   (2007), "Truth Commissions: State Terror, History, and Memory", *Radical History Review*, Vol. 97, Winter 2007.

Greenspan, Alan   (2007), *The Age of Turbulence*, London: Allen Lane.

Greenwood, Davydd J., and William A. Stinni   (1977), *Nature, Culture, and Human History*, New York: Harper and Row

Grenville, Kate   (2010), "A true apology to Aboriginal people means action as well", *The Guardian*, February 15.

Grevenbroek, Johannes Gulielmus de   (1958), "An Elegant and Accurate Account of the....Hottentots" (translated from Latin), cited in George (1958)

Guardian, The   (2009), "Fascism's shadow", London, March 30.

Guatemalan Commission for Historical Clarification   (2007), *Guatemala: Memory of Silence*, Report, 2007.

Guess, George M.   (1979), *Bureaucracy and the Unmanaged Forest Commons in Costa Rica*, Working Paper No. 1, Albuquerque: Latin American Institute, University of New Mexico.

Harrison, Fred   (1979), "Gronlund and Other Marxists", in R.V. Andelson (1979).

Harrison, Fred   (1983) *The Power in the Land*, London: Shepheard-Walwyn.

Harrison, Fred   (1986), *Brady & Hindley: Genesis of the Moors Murders*, Bath: Ashgrove Press.

Harrison, Fred   (1997), *The Chaos Makers*, London: Othila Press.

Harrison, Fred   (2005), *Boom Bust: House Prices, Banking and the Depression of 2010*, London: Shepheard-Walwyn (2nd edn 2007).

Harrison, Fred   (2006a), *Wheels of fortune: Self-funding Infrastructure and the Free Market Case for a Land Tax*, London: Institute of Economic Affairs.

Harrison, Fred   (2006b), *Ricardo's Law: House Prices and the Great Tax Clawback Scam*, London: Shepheard-Walwyn.

Harrison, Fred   (2008), *The Silver Bullet*, London: International Union.

Henley, Jon   (2007), "Bye-bye Belgium", *The Guardian*, November 13.

Hewetson, John   (1987), in Kropotkin 1987.

Hogg, David J. (2007), *Sir Arthur Lawley: Eloquent Knight Errant*,

Hogue, Arthur R. (1986), *Origins of the Common Law*, Indianapolis: Liberty Fund.

Holman, Federico, R.D. Estrada, F. Romero and L.E. Villegas (1992), "Technology Adoption and Competitiveness in Small Milk Producing farms in Costa Rica", *Livestock Research for Rural Development*, Vol. 4, July.

Holmes, Kim R., Edwin J. Feulner and Mary A. O'Grady (2008), *Index of Economic Freedom* Washington: Heritage Foundation/Dow Jones.

Hudson, Michael (2004), "The Development of Money-of-Account in Sumer's Temples", in Michael Hudson and Cornelia Wunsch, ed., *Creating Economic Order: Record-Keeping, Standardization and the Development of Accounting in the Ancient Near East*, Bethesda: CDL Press.

Hutchinson, Robert (2007), *Thomas Cromwell: The Rise and Fall of Henry VIII's most Notorious Minister*, London: Orion Books.

Ian Wright (1980), "Fiji prospers despite legacy of racial mix", *The Guardian*, October 10.

Institute for Economics & Peace (2009), *Peace, its Causes and Economic Value*, Sydney.

Jakobstein, Helen L. (1987), *The Process of Economic Development in Costa Rica, 1948-1970*, New York: Garland Publishing.

James, William (1926), *The Philosophy of William James* (Horace M. Kallen, ed.)., New York: Modern Library.

Jolly, Richard (2005), "Global inequality in historical perspective", UNU-WIDER Jubilee Conference, www.rrojasdatabank.info/widerconf/Jolly.pdf

Jupp, Kenneth (1997), *Stealing our Land*, London: Othila Press.

Kirby, Diane and Catherine Coleborne (2001), *Law, History, Colonialism: the Reach of Empire*, Manchester, Manchester University Press.

Kropotkin, Peter (1987), *Mutual Aid* (1902), London: Freedom Press.

Lam, Alven H.S. (2008), Ch. 19, in Andelson (2000).

Lawrence, Bruce B., and Aisha Karim (2007), *On Violence*, Durham: Duke University Press.

Lemarchand, René (1970), *Rwanda and Burundi*, London: Pall Mall Press.

Leslie, John (1978), *The Historical Development of the Indian Act*, Ottawa: Department of Indian Affairs and Northern Development, Treaties and Historical Research Branch.

Linotte, Daniel (2007), "Terrorism", in Lomborg (2007).

Lomborg. Bjørn (2007), *Solutions for the World's Biggest Problems*, Cambridge: Cambridge University Press.

Long, Edward (2002), *The History of Jamaica: Reflections on its Situation, Settlements, Inhabitants, Climate, Products, Commerce, Laws, and

BIBLIOGRAPHY

Government, London: T. Lowndes, 1774; reprinted by Ian Randle Publishers (Introduction, Howard Johnson).

Maitland, F.W. (1961), *The Constitutional History of England* (editor: H.A.L. Fisher), Cambridge: University Press.

Manners, Robert A. (1962), "Land Use, Labor, and Growth of Market Economy in Kipsigis Country", in Paul Bohannan and George Dalton (eds.), *Markets in Africa*, Evanston: Northwestern University Press.

Marx, Karl (1973a), "The Nationalisation of the Land", in *Selected Works*, Moscow: Progress Publishers, Vol. 2.

Marx, Karl (1973b), *Grundrisse*, Harmondsworth: Penguin.

Mason, Christopher (2008), "Canada says sorry for schools that tried to 'kill the Indian'", *Financial Times*, June 12.

Matusse, Renato (2004), *Guebuza: A Passion for the Land*, Maputo: Macmillan Mozambique.

McDowell, Christopher (ed.) (1996), *Understanding Impoverishment: the Consequences of Development-Induced Displacement*, Providence: Berghahn Books.

McGrath, Alistair (2007), *Christianity's Dangerous Idea: The Protestant Revolution*, London: SPCK.

McManis, Douglas R. (1964), *The Initial Evaluation and Utilisation of the Illinois Prairies, 1815-1840*, Chicago: University of Chicago.

Mehrotra, Santosh, and Richard Jolly (eds.) (1997), *Development With a Human Face*, Oxford: Clarendon Press.

Mehrotra, Santosh, In-Hwa Park and Hwa-Jong Baek (1997), "Social Policies in a Growing Economy: The Role of the State in the Republic of Korea", in Mehrotra and Jolly (1997).

Meredith, Martin (2007), *Mugabe: Power, Plunder, and the Struggle for Zimbabwe*, New York: Public Affairs.

Miller, George J. (2003), *Dying for Justice*, London: Centre for Land Policy Studies.

Milsom, S.F.C. (1981), *Historical Foundations of the Common Law*, London: Butterworths.

Moorhouse, Geoffrey (2008), *The Last Office: 1539 and the Dissolution of a Monastery*, London: Weidenfeld & Nicolson.

Morel, E.D. (2005), *Red Rubber: The Story of the Rubber Slave Trade Flourishing on the Congo in the Year of Grace 1906*, Reprint, Honolulu: University Press of the Pacific.

Niehoff, Debra (1999), *The Biology of Violence*, New York: The Free Press.

Oglesby, Elizabeth (2007), "Educating Citizens in Postwar Guatemala: Historical Memory, Genocide, and the Culture of Peace", in *Radical History Review* (97), Winter 2007.

Pappe, Ilan   (2006), *The Ethnic Cleansing of Palestine*, Oxford: Oneworld.

Peake, Harold   (1922), *The English Village: The Origin and Decay of its Community*, London: Benn Brothers.

Pennell, C.R.   (2000), *Morocco Since 1830*, London: Hurst.

Phang, Sock-Yong   (2000), Ch. 20 in Andelson (2000).

Pichot, André   (2009), *The Pure Society: From Darwin to Hitler*, London: Verso.

Pollock, Sir Frederick, and F.W. Maitland   (1968), *The History of English Law*, Cambridge: University Press

Rahman, Maseeh   (2008), "Land riots bring down Kashmir coalition", *The Guardian*, July 8.

Robertson, Robbie, and William Sutherland   (2001), *Government by the Gun: The Unfinished Business of Fiji's 2000 Coup*, Annendale, NSW: Pluto Press.

Rolbein, Seth   (1989), *Nobel Costa Rica*, New York: St. Martin's Press.

Sacks, Jonathan   (2007), *The Home We Build Together: Re-creating Society*, London: Continuum.

Salazar, Jorge Mario   (1981), *Politica y reforma en Costa Rica 1914-1958*, San José: Editorial Porvenir.

Schmitt, Carl   (2006), *The* Nomos *of the Earth*, New York: Telos Press.

Schore, Allan N.   (2003), "Early Relational Trauma, Disorganized Attachment, and the Development of a Pre-disposition to Violence", in Marion F. Solomon and Danielle J. Siegel, *Healing Trauma: attachment, mind, body, and brain*, New York: WW. Norton, 2003

Schumpeter, Joseph A.   (1954), *History of Economic Analysis*, London: Allen and Unwin.

Scornik-Gerstein, Fernando, and Fred Foldvary   (2010), *The Marginalists and the Special Status of Land as a Factor of Production*, London: theIU.

Seligson, M.A.   (1980), *Peasants of Costa Rica and the Development of Agrarian Capitalism*, Madison: University of Wisconsin Press.

Shaw, R. Paul   (1976), *Land Tenure and the Rural Exodus in Chile, Colombia, Costa Rica, and Peru*, Gainesville, FL: University Presses of Florida.

Spencer, Herbert   (1851), *Social Statics*; New York: Robert Schalkenbach Foundation, 1995.

Standing, Guy   (1978), "Basic needs and contrived stagnation in Guyana", *Caribbean Issues*, December.

Stephenson, Carl   (1954), *Mediaeval Institutions: Selected Essays* (Editor: Bryce D. Lyon), Ithaca: Cornell University Press.

Stepputat, Finn   (2007), "Forced Migration, Land & Sovereignty", Lecture, University of Oxford: Refugee Studies Centre, Nov. 21.

Stratton, Allegra   (2009), "Hodge renews warning to counter BNP threat", *The Guardian*, March 30.

BIBLIOGRAPHY

Taylor, Kathleen (2009), *Cruelty: Human Evil and the Human Brain*, Oxford: Oxford University Press.

Temple, C.L. (1918), *Native Races and Their Rulers: Sketches and Studies of Official Life and Administrative Problems in Nigeria*, Cape Town: Argus.

Tomlins, Christopher (2001), in Kirby and Coleborne (2001).

Traynor, Ian (2009), "MEPs move to deny extremist Jean-Marie Le Pen platform", *The Guardian*, March 26.

UNCTAD (2008), *The Least Developed Countries Report 2008*, New York: UN.

Vega Carballo, Jose Luis (1982), *hacia una interpretacion del desarrollo costaricense*, San Jose, CR: Editorial Porvenir.

Villanueva, Benjamin (1960), *An Approach to the Study of the Industrial Surplus: The Case of the United Fruit Company in Central America*, Madison Land Tenure Center, University of Wisconsin.

Vinogradoff, Sir Paul (1968), *Villainage in England* (1892), Oxford: Clarendon Press.

Wacker, Peter O. (1975), *Land and People: A Cultural Geography of Pre-industrial New Jersey*, New Brunswick: Rutgers University Press

Walker, Peter (2009), "Villagers swamped by second homes cheer vandals", *The Guardian*, March 21.

Ward-Perkins, Bryan (2005), *The Fall of Rome and the End of Civilisation*, Oxford: Oxford University Press

Weissart, Will (2008), "Castro gives private farmers space to grow", *The Guardian*, July 19.

White, Matthew (2001), *Historical Atlas of the Twentieth Century* http://users.erols.com/mwhite28/warstat2.htm

Wilson, Bruce M. (1998), Bruce M. Wilson. *Costa Rica: Politics, Economics and Democracy*, Boulder: Lynne Reiner.

Wily, Liz Alden (2003), *Land Rights in Crisis: Restoring Tenure Security in Afghanistan*, Kabul: Afghanistan Research and Evaluation Unit.

World Bank (1993), *Costa Rica and Uruguay: The Political Economy of Poverty, Equity, and Growth* (Simon Rottenberg, ed.), Oxford: Oxford University Press.

World Bank (1994), *Resettlement and Development: the Bankwide Review of Projects Involving Involuntary Resettlement 1986-1993*, Washington DC: The Environment Department.

Wright, John *Libya*, London: Ernest Benn, 1969.

Zoomers, Annalies, and Gemma van der Haar (2000) (eds.), *Current Land Policy in Latin America: Regulating Land Tenure Under Neo-liberalism*, Amsterdam: Royal Tropical Institute.

About the Author

FRED HARRISON studied economics at Oxford, first at Ruskin College and then at University College, where he read Politics, Philosophy and Economics.

His MSc is from the University of London. Following a career in Fleet Street, he embarked on a 10-year sojourn in Russia, following the collapse of Communism, in what turned out to be a fruitless bid to help the people to avoid the adoption of the economics favoured by the Predators. Boris Yeltsin wouldn't listen, and the country was delivered to the oligarchs.

INDEX

Abu Ghraib Prison, 147
Abyssinia, 81
Afghanistan, viii, x, 83,91-94
Africa, 39. 65, 96, 153
   infrastructure, xi
   land grabs and, xiii, 102
Ahmida, Ali Abdullatif, 98, 102
Algiers, 61
Al-Qaeda, x
Ameringer, Charles, 31
Anarchy, 54, 75, 77
ANC, 140, 142, 143
Angola, 66
Apartheid, 137, 140-141
Appa, Gautam, 109
Arbenz, Jacobo, 139
Arendt, Hannah, 148
Argentina, 131, 136, 150
Aristocracy, 28
Ashdown, Lord (Paddy), 91
Athens, 61
Australia, 72, 105, 136, 137, 142, 152

Basque, 21
Belgium, 118
Bengal, 135-136
Bidwell, Robin, 59
Blair, Tony, 94
Botswana, 149
Brady, Ian, 25
Brazil, 84, 131, 150
Brendon, Piers, 108
Bridgetower, George, 67
British South African Company, 88
Brown, Gordon, xiii
Bush, George W., xvii, 94

Caesar, Julius, 60
Campbell-Scott, Duncan, 48
Canada, 48, 58, 136, 137
Capitalism, 9,49, 72, 149
   land grabbing and, viii
   organised violence and, 13, 69,
   pathology and, viii, x, 10-12
   predators and, viii, x, 10-12, 70, 156

producers and, 12-13
    See: Imperialism,
Cernia, Michael, 108
Chagos Islands, 19
Chile, 131, 132, 136
CIA, 94, 139
Collier, Paul, 38
Colombia, 131, 132
Colonialism, 30, 31, 44, 47, 90, 102, 107, 109, 136, 153
    land grabbing and, xii, 19, 43, 45, 48, 57, 71-73, 80, 86, 91
    See: Neo-colonialism,
Columbus, Christopher, 33
Communism, ix, 69
Communist Party (Costa Rica), 124
Community Land Trust, 141-144
Concentration camps, 72-74
Congo, 75
Co-operation, 4, 155
Costa Rica, 29-39, 149-153
    infrastructure and , 30, 122
    See: United Fruit Company,
Covenant: see: land,
Crane, Mark, 39
Culture, 3-4, 8, 17, 18, 26, 34, 98, 137
    rent and, 10, 19

Darwin, Charles, 147
Day, David, 57
Democracy, Xii
Democratic Kampuchea, 60
Dominican Republic, 150
Durkheim, Emile, xiii

Economics , 21, 152
    classical , ix, 6
    post-classical, viii, xvi
Economics & Peace, Institute for, 152
Economist Intelligence Unit, 23
Ecuador, 131
Edelman, Marc, 128
Egalitarianism, 5, 7, 11, 30, 36, 65, 125, 129
Einstein, Albert, 26
Ekin, Des, 61
El Salvador, 30, 35, 131
Enlightenment, The, xiii, 63
Ethiopia, 97
Evans-Pritchard, E.E., 98-100

Failed States, 27, 29, 83, 94, 96
Fascism, ix, 13, 95-103, 148
Ferrer, Don José Figueres, 31
Financial Times, The, 135
Fiscal freedom, 126-134
Flores, Alfredo Gonzáles, 127
Foreign aid, 39
Foucault, Michel, 26
France, 21, 59, 103
Freeman, Edward, 43
Freud, Sigmund, 26

Gaddafi, Muammar, 102-103
Geldof, Bob, xi
Genocide, 17, 39, 59, 69-80, 91, 115, 139, 147, 148
George, Henry, 127
George, Katherine, 65

INDEX

Girouard, Sir Percy, 50
Govan, Fiona, 105
Governance, non-violent, 147-156
Graziani, Rodolfo, 73, 101
Great Depression (1930s), 23, 28, 96
Greenspan, Alan, 94
Grenville, Kate, 137
Grevenbroek, Johannes Gulielmus de, 65
Guatemala, 30, 36, 52-53, 131, 138, 139
Guyana, 83

Hague, The, 75, 148
Hardenburg, Walter, 59
Heiser, Victor, 80
Henry VIII, 11, 19, 114
Himalayas, 22
Hitler, Adolf, 26, 58, 95, 117, 148
Hobson, J.A., 49
Hogg, David, 73
Holocaust, 24
Honduras, 30, 36
Hoyte, Desmond, 87
Hussain, Saddam, xi
Hut Tax, 51, 79

Idris, King, 103
ILO, 84
IMF, 149-152
Imperialism, 49
India, 54, 85, 105, 108, 122, 125-126, 127, 134
Infrastructure,
Iraq, vii, 94, 105

Ireland (North), 115, 117
Islam, 102-104, 156
    Sanusiya, 99
    suicide bombers and, 27, 105-106, 107
Israel, 110, 155
Italy, 25, 28, 73, 95, 98-102, 117

Jamaica, 62-68, 123-124
James, William, xi
Jefferson, Thomas, 34, 121, 124
Jerusalem, 110
Jesus, 153
Johnston, Sir Harry, 79
Jubilee, year of, 118
Jupp, Sir Kenneth, 114

Kashmir, 55, 115
Keith, Henry Meiggs, 122-123
Kenya, 50-51, 115
Kropotkin, Peter, 147, 154

Land, x, 25, 37, 45, 84-85, 88, 100, 118, 132, 140-145, 153
    covenant and, 110, 117
    landless, 18, 36
    prices, xv, 22, 150-151
    privatisation and, xiii, xiv, 11, 12, 19, 52, 104, 116, 155
    property rights and, 3, 4, 6, 33, 46, 50, 63-64, 72, 76-77, 93, 97, 121, 123, 136, 149, 153
    social pathology and, 16-17, 21, 157-138, 155
    speculation, 22, 23, 47, 125, 150-151
    sprawl, 22

urban markets and, 94, 133, 151
See also: Land tax; Jubilee, year of;
  Violence,
Land grant colleges, 114 n.3, 143 n.3
Land tax , 77, 89, 123, 126-134, 151
Le Pen, Jean Marie, 148
Lemarchand, René, 76-79
Lenape, 46
Lenin, V.I., 49, 72
Leopold II, King, 75, 79-80
Libya, 97
Linotte, Daniel, xiv
Locke, John, 121
Long, Edward, 62-68

Madison, James, 121
Mafia, x, 17, 28
Maoism, 72, 135, 153
Marx, Karl, 17, 70-72
Marxism, 25, 71, 84, 87, 89, 96, 124, 138
Mashonaland, 87-88
Matabeleland, 88, 90
Mauritius, 19
McManis, Douglas, 47
Mexico, 29, 54
Monge, Luis Alberto, 32
Morel, E.D., 79
Morocco, 59, 104-106
Moses, 111, 117
Movement for Democratic Change, 90
Mozambique, 138, 141
Mugabe, Robert, xiii, 89-90, 144
Multi-culturalism, 112, 144
Mussolini, Benito, 25, 28, 95, 98-101

Namibia, 59
NATO, 33, 118
Natural rights, 8, 148
Naxalites,
Nazi Germany, 24, 58, 59, 95, 148
Neo-colonialism, 32, 49, 77-78
Neuro-science, 23, 62, 155
Nicaragua, 30
Nigeria, 72
Nkomo, Joshua, 89-90

Obama, Barack, vii, viii, x, xi, 41, 149
Organised crime, 28
Ottoman Empire, 97, 102

Pakistan, vii, 29, 107
  infrastructure and, viii, x
Palestine, 110, 155
Pauperisation, 13, 15-25
Peace Dividend, 38-39, 152
People's Democratic Party of
  Afghanistan, 92
Peru, 131, 132
Pilger, John, 119
Post, Louis F., 127
Predators *See:* Capitalism,
Producers *See:* Capitalism,
Provisional IRA, 118

Racism *See:* Edward Long,
Religion, 105-106
  fundamentalism, 17, 29
Rent, viii, x, 7, 8, 11, 19, 21, 34, 85, 94,
  115, 143, 154

INDEX

oil, xiv 91, 94
   rent-seeking, 20, 24, 86, 91, 106, 127
Rhodes, Cecil, 87
Rome, 9, 61, 99. 100
Roosevelt, Theodore, 59
Rudd, Kevin, 137
Rwanda, 60, 75-80, 115, 136

Sacks, Jonathan, 111-118
Sand Creek Massacre, 136-137
Schmitt, Carl, 44-49
Schumpeter, Joseph, 27
Schweitzer, Albert, 1
Selznick, Philip, 112
Senegal, 66
Shaw, Paul, 132
Sierra Leone, 39, 136
Slavery, 61, 63, 67, 83
Smith, Adam, xvi
Smith, Ian, 88
Social contract, 112, 115, 153
Social universe, 4, 8, 15, 21
Socialism, 86, 87, 90, 96, 99
Sociogenic, ix
Somalia, 155
South Africa, xiii, 73, 136, 140-145
Spain, 21, 33, 44, 65, 74, 103
Spencer, Herbert, 43
Stalin, Joseph, 24
Standing, Guy, 84
Suicide bombers See: Islam,
Supplanting societies, 55, 57-62

Taliban, 91, 92

Taxation, 27, 30, 51, 79, 85, 95, 104, 133, 151
   Iron Law of, xv
   pricing mechanism, 153-155
   progressive, 129
   violence and, 24, 28, 77, 124
   See: Hut Tax; Fiscal freedom,
Taylor, Kathleen, 59, 62, 155
Temple, C.I., 72
Tenure, rights of, 16, 20
Territoriality, xii, 4, 75
Terrorism, 39
Tetouan, 105
Transport, 108, 124-126
   land values and, 122-123, 151-152
Trauma thinking, xiv-xvi
Truth and Reconciliation Commissions, 136
Tsvangerai, Morgan, 90
Tutu, Desmond, xiii, 111, 136

UNICEF, 153
United Fruit Company, 37, 38, 123-127
United Nations, 91, 121
USA , 29, 30, 91, 93, 136, 139
USAID, 139
USSR, 91, 92, 93, 139, 153
Utopianism, 17
Utrecht, Treaty of, 61

Venezuela, 84, 150
Violence, viii, 3, 20, 25, 38, 46, 104, 107, 137, 138, 145
   capitalism and, vii, 13
   land and, viii, 12, 53, 55, 66, 87, 152

language and, vii, viii, 15, 18, 62-68, 138-139
organised, viii, xi-xiv, 8, 22, 24, 122, 135
systemic, 108, 118, 148, 156
taxation and, xi
See: Organised crime,
Wages, 6, 7, 11, 34
Wakefield, Edward Gibbon, 72
Walras, León, xvi
War: see Peace Dividend,
Warlordism, 91, 118

Washington Consensus, The, 35, 149, 152
White, Matthew, 69
Wilson, Woodrow, 127
Wily, Liz, 92-93
World Bank, 33-34, 108, 109, 125, 129, 130
Wright, John, 96, 101

Zimbabwe, xiii, 83, 115, 117, 141, 144, 154
Zone of Violence , 30
Zoomers. Annelies, 133